Don't Throw It Away!

alphabet building blocks
apple basket
barrel, wooden
beads
bedslat
belt
birth announcement
bleach bottle, white plastic
bottle caps with fluted edges
box, wooden, with lid
bread and butter spreader
bread board
broom handle
buttons
can, metal, aluminum
can, metal, with lid
can, tuna fish
candles, pieces of
candy jar, glass
cardboard, shirt
cigar box, wooden
clothespin, pinch type
coat hanger, wire
coffee can, 1-pound, with plastic lid
coffee can, 3-pound
cookie can top
cornucopia
dowels, wooden
drapery ring, wooden
drawer, desk
drawer pull
driftwood
earring
egg carton, plastic
egg shells
fabric
film containers
fishing tackle box
flashlight lens

flower, plastic
food containers, plastic
frozen pudding containers
gift wrapping paper
greeting card
hand mirror
hardware cloth
hat, woman's, soft straw
instant coffee jar, 2-ounce
insulation board
ironing board, wooden
jewelry
jigsaw puzzle
key chain
kitchen grater
lamp shade
lid, plastic, from can of coffee
liquor bottle
liquor bottle screw-on cap
lumber, scrap
luncheon mats, straw
magazine
meat grinder
military boot
milk carton, cardboard
mirror frame
mirror glass
mop handle
mug (for coffee)
napkin, party
newspaper
olive pits
packing straw
panty hose
paper bag, heavy-duty
peach pits
pearls
phonograph lid
picture frame

pictures from books and catalogs
pill bottle, plastic
placemat
plate, clear glass
pocketbook handle
postage stamps
produce boxes, plastic
rhinestones
salad bowl
salad bowl, wooden
sandwich bags, plastic
screening, heavy-duty
sea shells
sewing spools, wooden
shoe box, plastic-coated
shopping bag with design
silver chest, wooden
six-pack carrying handles, plastic
skillet, aluminum
soda pop can, aluminum
soda pop can, zip-off ring
split peas
spray can
spray can top
starfish
stockings, nylon
table leg, wooden
tea kettle, rusted
tomato basket, cardboard
wallpaper
washboard
washcloth
wastepaper basket, metal
wedding gift wrapping paper
wedding invitation
window shade roller
window shade runner
wine bottle labels
wood, scrap

Don't Throw It Away!

Vivian Abell

CHL CREATIVE HOME LIBRARY®
In Association with Better Homes and Gardens
Meredith Corporation

CHL CREATIVE HOME LIBRARY®

© 1973 by Meredith Corporation, Des Moines, Iowa
All rights reserved
Printed in the United States of America
First Edition Third Printing, 1975

Library of Congress Cataloging in Publication Data.
Abell, Vivian.
Don't throw it away!
1. Handicraft. I. Title.
TT157.A23   745.5   73-7844
ISBN 0-696-19100-8

Contents

About the Author

Vivian Abell has been involved with craft for 25 years—as artist, teacher, and retail dealer. She entered the retail business several years ago because she couldn't find the supplies she needed for her own craft work. The store she owns—Craft Town in Verona, New Jersey—is one of the best in the country from the standpoint of quality goods. Twenty different craft classes are conducted there each week, attended by more than 250 women, men, and children. Vivian also teaches craft in the Montclair, New Jersey, adult school system, and she is co-hostess of a TV show, "All about Crafts." In 1972 she was a judge for national decoupage and egg decorating contests. Although Vivian is talented in all crafts, her favorite is three-dimensional decoupage.

Preface

Nowadays the ecologists and anti-pollution experts tell us not to throw things away. I've instinctively followed that advice all my life. I've saved tin cans, bottles, scrap lumber, and other discards—my own as well as other people's. I hope my friends and neighbors who have considered me a bit of a character for many years recognize now that I've never been anything but a patriotic, responsible, ecology-minded citizen. These friends have often peered into my car to see what peculiar objects were on the back seat—perhaps a stack of dried straw, a rusty meat grinder, an old washboard.

I've had a magpie bent ever since I was a small child. My mother had natural artistic flair. She was always in charge of decorations for every organization to which she belonged. And I tagged after her picking up scraps from which to make something. Yet when a school aptitude test indicated I had artistic leanings, I thought it highly amusing because I couldn't draw a thing. (I still can't draw today!) Besides, I had already made up my mind to become a nurse.

My nursing career ended when I married one of my patients, Dunbar Abell. I found it especially exciting in those early years of marriage, when income was sparse, to decorate our home with things one might normally throw away. The effects I achieved were not only unusual, they were downright handsome. After our three children were born, I became even more involved with crafts. In addition to decorating for holidays and parties, I started teaching crafts to children in local scout troops, and because there was always such a mini-budget, I resorted more and more to crafts made from throwaways.

My career in crafts grew. With my husband's encouragement, I opened Craft Town in 1969. The shop carries craft supplies and offers courses in every kind of craft. Then in 1971 I was asked to co-host a television program, "All about Crafts," which today is shown in several major cities. These experiences have given me great happiness, for I love crafts and the people involved with crafts, many of whom have helped me along the way. For example, without the wonderful staff in my shop I could never have managed the time to do the television series or this book. I am especially grateful to Mary Pat Evans.

Over the years my husband kept urging me to put my craft ideas in writing, especially my ideas about making decorative, useful things out of throwaway materials. The television series reinforced his belief that many people find the "don't throw it away" approach very appealing. Whenever I did a show based on throwaways, I received many, many letters.

It is immensely satisfying for me to realize how my life has come full circle. I went into nursing because I wished to help care for people. I went into crafts to fill the years when family needs kept me housebound. And I discovered in crafts what sent me into nursing in the first place: the joy of watching people come alive.

Everyone has an urge to create something; I am sure this explains the present explosion of interest in crafts. Children develop a growing confidence when they produce something with a few supplies and a little direction. Busy adults find that making something with their hands provides a refreshing change of pace from the pressures of daily life. Older people—perhaps retired—find renewed life in being happily busy with a new hobby.

And in don't-throw-it-away crafts, people are doubly pleased when they can make an exciting new possession from what would have been a discard. There's a special satisfaction in making something from almost nothing or turning an old eyesore into a useful, attractive object.

This book has been written for Dunny, my beloved late husband, who shared the fun and the dreams that went into it.

Upper Montclair, New Jersey   —Vivian Abell
1973

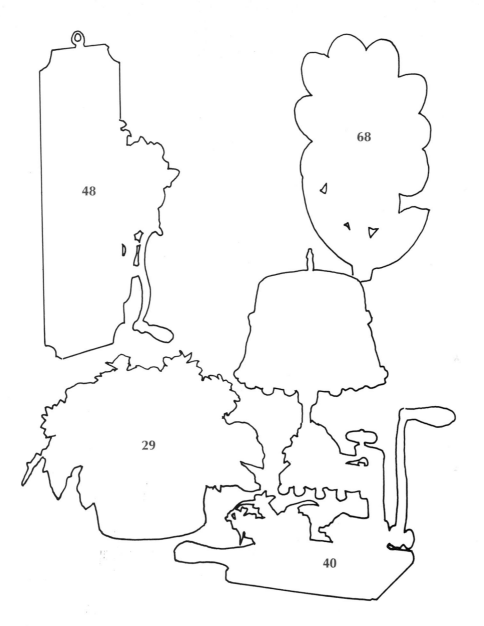

Details and instructions for projects shown may be found on page number indicated

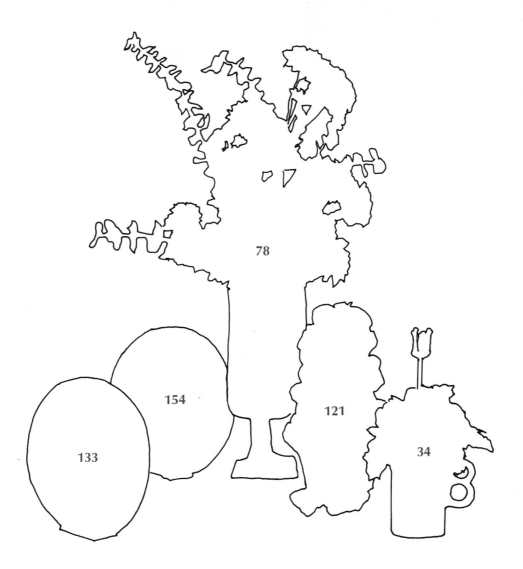

Details and instructions for projects shown may be found on page number indicated

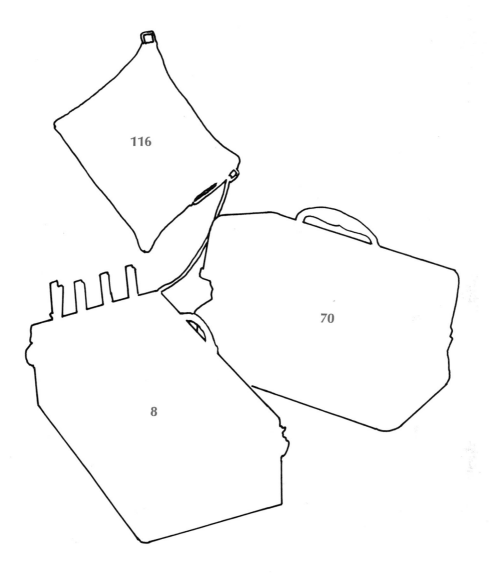

Details and instructions for projects shown may be found on page number indicated

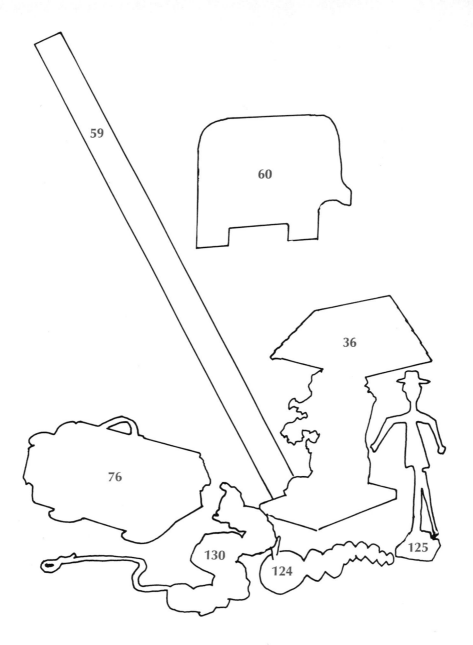

Details and instructions for projects shown may be found on page number indicated

I
Never Forget
To Hang Up
My Clothes

Introduction

Just as love alone will not ensure happiness in life, it is also not enough to ensure success in craft. In addition to the desire to make something beautiful or useful, you need the materials to execute your idea and the proper tools to complete your project. I have seen craft lovers frustrated by the loss of valuable time and even by the ruination of a project because they had to stop to search for needed tools in the midst of their work.

Moreover, much as I love it, craft work is sometimes messy work. You can't really lose yourself totally in a craft project if you are worried about protecting your clothing.

Consequently, there are two things I always teach in my craft classes.

1. You should have a special craft workbasket filled with those items you use over and over in your craft projects.
2. You should protect your good clothing with a smock or apron.

I don't mean by this that it's necessary to go out and purchase an elaborate workbasket or a designer smock. A man's shirt that is a bit too shabby for wear makes an excellent smock for craft. If you sew, you can make an attractive and inexpensive smock from leftover fabric or a damaged sheet.

Each year in my adult school classes, I offer a prize for the most original workbasket. Picnic hampers, baskets with handles, and sturdy boxes decorated with paint, wallpaper, gift wrapping paper, and leftover fabric all vie with one another for the award of being the most creative. My students have produced some truly beautiful workbaskets, but my favorite is a cardboard tomato basket with a wooden handle, an item frequently thrown away in the produce section of grocery stores. Here are the directions for making it. (See completed project on page 4.)

Materials

cardboard tomato basket, 7½ inches × 15 inches, with wooden handle

gesso

#220 sandpaper

instant decoupage (Fun Podge, Mod Podge, Decollage)

brayer

leftover fabric to cover outside and inside of basket (for outside: cotton, burlap, adhesive paper, wallpaper, gift wrapping paper; for inside: vinyl, adhesive paper)

ribbon to go around basket and handle

pinch clothespins

trim to go around basket and handle

Procedure

1. Inspect the basket to make sure there are no breaks. Apply one coat gesso around the bottom and 4 sides of the basket (to reinforce, and prevent the color of the grower's printing from showing through the fabric). Allow to dry. Sand lightly.

2. Apply one coat instant decoupage over entire basket, concentrating on one side at a time. Allow to dry. On newspaper draw a pattern to the dimensions of the basket and cut out. Place the pattern on your fabric, planning to use your fabric pattern to the best advantage; plan to match your fabric where necessary. Cut out 2 pieces of fabric for sides according to the pattern, plus ¾-inch overlap at each end and at the bottom; keep the top flush with the basket top. Cut out 2 pieces of fabric for the ends of the basket according to the pattern, allowing ¾-inch overlap at the bottom and keeping the top and sides flush. Cut out a piece of fabric for the outside bottom of the basket, keeping all edges flush.

3. Continue to work on one panel at a time. Apply one coat instant decoupage to the back of the fabric and to a 15-inch side of the basket. Apply fabric to the basket, allowing the overlap where indicated; roll out with a brayer from the center to the 4 corners of the fabric, making sure to roll out all air bubbles. Wipe brayer frequently to remove excess finish. Repeat the procedure on the other 15-inch side, the 2 end pieces, and the bottom piece. Clean the brayer well with soap and water when finished. Allow basket to dry completely.

4. Cut down your newspaper pattern to fit the inside basket dimensions of the 4 sides. Cut out the inside lining exactly the same way as the outside lining, matching your fabric and allowing the same overlap. Repeat the procedure for application. (If you have a long piece of fabric, you can go around the 4 sides of the basket with just one seam at a corner, still keeping the top flush and allowing the ¾-inch bottom overlap.)

5. Cut down your newspaper pattern to fit the inside bottom of the basket. Cut a piece of cardboard slightly smaller than your newspaper pattern to allow for the bulk of fabric overlap. Cut the fabric according to the newspaper pattern, allowing a ¾-inch overlap on all 4 sides of the bottom piece. Place the fabric around the cardboard; fit before gluing to be sure the lining will not pucker, and trim the cardboard a little if it does not fit. Glue the back of the fabric to the top of the cardboard; overlap and glue the additional ¾-inch allowance to the back of the cardboard. Glue the fabric-covered cardboard to the inside basket bottom. (If the bottom lining of the basket gets dirty, you can change it by lifting out the fabric-covered cardboard, and putting in a new bottom lining.) When dry, brush a coat of instant decoupage over the bottom lining fabric. Allow basket to dry thoroughly.

6. Glue ribbon around the top edges of the basket, folding equally over the inside and outside edges. On both 15-inch sides of the basket, clip the ribbon on the inside lining side in 2 places, at either end of the handle, to permit the ribbon to lie flat. Clip the ribbon at each of the 4 corners on the basket lining side; mitre the inside corners, or cut away excess ribbon bulk. If you used small pieces of leftover ribbon, you may have to cut your ribbon in 4 pieces; butt outside corners and mitre inside edges. Use pinch clothespins to hold glued ribbon edges tightly in place until glue dries. If you are using velveteen ribbon, place strips of cardboard between the clothespins and the ribbon so that the velveteen does not mark.

7. Glue ribbon to the basket handle. If your ribbon is wide enough to cover front and back of handle, center it on the top side of the handle and fold it around to meet on the underside. If ribbon will not go all the way around the handle, glue a strip of ribbon on the underside of the handle; place another piece of ribbon on the top side and fold it around the handle to overlap the ribbon underneath.

8. Glue trim around the outside of the basket at the point where the ribbon and the fabric meet.

Once you have a workbasket, fill it up with those materials you will always need to have on hand. Although the list is a formidable one, you already have some of the items in your home. Others are quite inexpensive or easily secured. And what you don't have, you can add as your needs and finances permit.

Here is an alphabetical listing of what a well-equipped workbasket should contain:

aluminum foil
awl (keep point covered with a piece of cork)
brayer (this is a small rubber roller)
burnisher
cheesecloth

cotton gloves, rubber gloves, or throwaway plastic
    gloves
decoupage scissors or manicure scissors
epoxy glue
eraser
florist tape, green
hammer
hand cleaner
ice pick (keep point covered with a piece of
    cork)
long-nosed pliers (optional, but useful)
masking tape
measuring tape
nails and screws, assortment
notebook
paintbrushes in several different sizes and
    several hobby brushes
paper clips
paper cups or juice can to hold paintbrushes
paper towels
pencils
pinch clothespins
Plasti-tak
rubber bands
ruler
sandpaper, #220, #400, #600, and sanding
    block
scissors, large and small
screwdriver
serrated knife or X-acto knife (keep point
    covered with a piece of Styrofoam)
sponge
steel wool, #0000
Stickum
Styrofoam
tack cloth
toothbrush, old
toothpicks
tweezers
U-pins, T-straight pins, or small hairpins
Velverette Craft Glue
waxed paper
white glue (clear-drying type, such as Sobo Glue
    or Bond Cement)
wire, fine
wire cutter
wooden craft sticks (don't throw away Popsicle
    sticks!)

There are several other items I usually keep in my workbasket because I use them so frequently: gesso; an antiquing product; a protective instant decoupage (such as Decollage, Fun Podge, Mod Podge); a spray varnish; acrylic spray; instant decoupage spray; some cans of stain; and a decoupage sealer. Your list of "extras" will depend on the particular craft that catches your fancy.

Craft stores are springing up across the country, so that the materials recommended for your workbasket (and needed for the various projects in this book) should not be hard to find. Still, it is quite possible that you may not know where craft materials are sold in your locale. If you need to know the craft store nearest you, simply address your query to Jack Wax, Profitable Hobby Merchandising, Inc., 444 Bedford Road, Pleasantville, New York 10570. But before you write Mr. Wax, be sure to check your local department stores for a craft department in them. In response to popular demand, many general merchandise stores have created departments devoted to craft materials.

Now that your workbasket is well equipped, you may be wondering about where to find, and even build, a collection of throwaway materials for the projects in this book. In ever so many places. Check your own basement, attic, and closets for things you no longer use for one reason or another. Look along the curb on trash collection day, or watch newspaper announcements for a town or neighborhood cleanup. Read your local newspaper for garage sales, porch sales, house sales, and farm sales. Support P.T.A., church, and club fundraising affairs. Visit flea markets, thrift shops, used furniture stores, Salvation Army stores, Goodwill shops. Let your friends know you want "don't-throw-it-away" objects. They'll bring you things they don't know how to use. (And if you make them something from what they've brought, you'll cement a friendship permanently.)

Many lumberyards will let you have cutting scraps, particularly if you're working for a fundraising organization. Wallpaper stores may be happy to give you old sample books, if you request them, and department stores might let you have their old greeting card sample books. An upholstery shop or a friend who sews might save you fabric scraps. Supermarkets have used wooden crates and produce baskets. There are many sources of free or inexpensive materials if you look around you.

Here are several more suggestions. Acquaint yourself with professional furniture stripping shops in your area. They can save you hours of work when it's necessary to strip old finishes from used furniture before applying new finishes. Familiarize yourself with, and keep abreast of, new craft materials and tools. Manufacturers are constantly coming up with new products that will make your work easier. Since this book was started, I've changed procedures on some of the projects either because I found a better product to use or I learned a better technique. Finally, get acquainted with your local craft shop, if there is one, and ask for advice as you need it. You will find knowledgeable, trained people there who are happy to answer questions and share with you the excitement and fun of your particular craft.

TIPS AND TRICKS

My steady participation in various crafts over the years has taught me numerous shortcuts, improved methods of doing things, and "nice to know," general tips to keep in mind when working at any craft. I feel this book would not be complete if I didn't share with my readers some of the discoveries I've made. Let me urge you always to refer to this section before beginning any project to see if any tips and tricks can be applied to that project.

Refinishing
● To prepare old wood for refinishing or to remove wax, wipe the wood with household ammonia (do not wash it). Wear rubber gloves and work outdoors, if possible.
● To remove lacquer from wood, make a paste of olive oil and flour. Apply with a soft dry cloth, then rub with a circular motion. Wipe off paste and polish wood with an old nylon stocking.
● Damaged areas in wood can be repaired by applying a liquid or solid wax filler, applying a thin coat of hard paste wax, and rubbing well with a piece of flannel.
● To clean and shine fine wooden furniture, prepare a mixture of ⅓ vinegar, ⅓ turpentine, and ⅓ boiled linseed oil. Apply with a damp cloth, and wipe off well to prevent darkening from the linseed oil.
● Scrap wood can be painted without stripping old finishes if you apply gesso to the wood and sand when dry; apply another coat of gesso, let dry, and sand again.

Paints and Sprays
● You should introduce yourself to acrylic paint. It is fast-drying, comes in a variety of colors, and the brushes are easily cleaned with water.
● You can mix your own acrylic paint to obtain variety in color. Experiment with your paints; there are enormous varieties in color, and often several ways to achieve them. Some of the possible color mixtures are:

pink = red + white
hot pink = thalo crimson + white
peach = cadmium red light + white
brick red = red + raw umber
flesh = burnt sienna + white
      or *yellow ochre + red + white*
orange = yellow + cadmium red light
gold = yellow ochre light + white
      or *cadmium yellow medium +*
            burnt sienna
green = blue + yellow
olive green = hookers green + brown +
  yellow + white
aqua = thalo green + white
turquoise = manganese blue + thalo green
purple = blue + red
lavender = purple + white
brown = red + orange
      or *yellow + blue + red*
      or *burnt sienna + black*
beige = brown + white
gray = white + black
ivory = white + yellow
      or *white + burnt umber*
           + yellow ochre

● Baby food jars are good for holding water and for mixing large amounts of paint for decorative painting.
● A cotton swab is helpful for getting paint into small areas.
● Old toothbrushes can be used to apply gesso and paints to ornate corners and moldings.
● It is no longer necessary to use red metal paint under gold leaf; use any color you wish.
● To conserve paint when you are working with good raw wood, apply a heavy coat of sealer before beginning to paint. (This is one of the rare times I'll recommend applying a heavy coat of anything.) For decorative painting of new wood, many people prefer a gesso base.
● When using a spray product, read the instructions carefully, then shake the container well. Hold the can 12 inches from the surface to be sprayed;

move the can from left to right and spray lightly, repeating until all areas are covered. Then start at the top and lightly spray to the bottom until all areas are covered.

- Use sprays in well-ventilated areas. Spraying into a cardboard box helps to keep the spray confined.
- In using any spray product, several misty coats are better than one heavy coat.
- Spray can tops are useful when you are using spray paint and want the paint in certain areas only. Spray a small amount of paint from the aerosol container into the lid, and brush on the paint wherever you wish.
- You can make a brush-on product become a spray product by using a Preval Multi-Purpose Spraymaker Power Unit and Preval bottle. The bottle can be cleaned and reused.
- Do not rush drying time; this can ruin the most carefully finished craft project. Allow adequate drying time *between* coats of anything, too. To test a finish for dryness, place a thumb or knuckle on the surface; if an indentation appears, allow additional drying time.
- Metal in good condition can be prepared for painting by washing the metal in a solution of vinegar and water.
- Before painting metal with acrylic paint, brush on a base coat of oil paint.

Staining and Antiquing
- Both sides of a piece of wood must be stained to prevent warping.
- The back of a stained wooden plaque should be covered with fabric, felt, wallpaper, or adhesive paper to prevent the stain from bleeding through to the wall.
- To make a metallic wax stain, add 1 part of a metallic wax (Treasure Jewels, Lustre Wax, Rub 'n Buff, Treasure Gold) to 1 part turpentine to 2 parts varnish. Mix in a plastic oleomargarine container.
- You can make your own antiquing glaze by mixing 3 tablespoons turpentine and 1½ teaspoons raw umber (or any other oil color you wish to use as an accent color in antiquing). When well mixed, add 3 tablespoons clear varnish.
- Textured paper towels are better than plain paper towels for removing antiquing glaze. The texture adds lines and character to your antiquing finish.
- Coarse hair nets (the type used by hairdressers) provide beautiful graining when used in antiquing.

Ask the hairdresser to save old ones for you.
- An old toothbrush is useful in "spatter antiquing" to create the tiny dots you see in commercially antiqued furniture. Dampen the brush with dark antiquing glaze or black acrylic paint, stand back from the surface to be antiqued, and flick your fingers or the edge of a knife across the bristles.
- In antiquing gold decoupage braid, pat off the excess antiquing with soft facial tissues (not paper towels, which can remove the color).
- The easiest way to paint the inside of a glass container is to pour glass stain inside the bottle and rotate until the paint covers the entire area.
- Do not use glass stain inside a glass container intended for use with food because some stains contain lead.
- To paint the outside of a glass container, apply glass stain generously and spread quickly with a brush or cotton swab.
- Small amounts of glass stain in a dark color can be swirled with a toothpick over a container painted with light-colored glass stain to create an unusual texture.

Brushes
- Brushes will last longer if you have a variety of brushes, and label them for repeated use with specific products; for example, use a varnish brush only for varnish and a gesso brush only for gesso. Write the product name with indelible India ink on masking tape and put it on the brush handle.
- Learn to clean brushes properly, as follows. Brushes used for water-based acrylic or latex paint: soap and water; brushes used for shellac: denatured alcohol; brushes used with oil paint or varnish: turpentine; brushes used to apply acrylic decoupage finishes: lacquer thinner.
- Store brushes in a container with the bristles upright.
- An old glass baby bottle is useful for holding varnish or lacquer brushes between applications of the finish. Cut off the top of the nipple and insert the brushes so that bristle ends are down. Put enough turpentine or lacquer thinner in the bottle to cover the bristles. Keep the brush in this solution between coats of finish.
- Tall olive jars are good for soaking thin brushes used for painting.
- You can renew brushes that have been washed or soaked in a cleansing agent by brushing the bristles back and forth lightly across a bar of soap,

and then reshaping the bristles with your fingers.
• If you are using varnish with some degree of frequency, your brush will last longer if you do not clean it after each use. Put the brush either in aluminum foil or a plastic bag, and put it in the freezer. Before re-using, allow time to defrost.

Varnishes, Lacquers, and Finishes
• Because varnish and lacquer deteriorate with age, it is better to buy small quantities and replace frequently.
• Be sure you have enough finish to complete a single project. Some finishes are not chemically compatible with other finishes.
• Never shake a can of brush-on decoupage finish or wipe a brush on the side of the can; you will create bubbles that will not disappear in the finish or in the brush.
• If you keep a straight pin near a can of lacquer, you can use it to lift off a lacquer bubble that might become imbedded in the finish if brushed.
• To remove lacquer from metal, wash the metal with turpentine, mineral spirits, or ammonia.
• Do not store varnish or lacquer in an outdoor garage in a cold climate as freezing will create problems in your finish.

Decoupage, Decorative Painting, and Repoussé
• In painting wood for decoupage or decorative painting, start the paint in the middle and brush out toward either end.
• Cardboard from hosiery, shirts, and gift boxes can be used to elevate cutouts in decorative painting and decoupage, or as a filler in lining pocketbooks with fabric.
• To sand the edges of a small cutout, use an emery board.
• To distress a print for decoupage, rip (do not cut) the edges; hold the print face up and tear the edges toward you to achieve a fine feathered edge. If you wish, you can age the print by wiping coffee on the edges. You can further distress the print by burning the edges with a match, or a cigarette.
• When gluing a print to a surface, sponge the back of the print with water before applying glue. The glue will then spread evenly, and the print will not wrinkle.
• To apply glue to small areas, squirt a small amount of glue on a piece of plastic or aluminum foil, then apply with a toothpick or cotton swab.

• Creases from folding in gift wrapping paper or wedding invitations can be carefully ironed out on the wrong side with a barely damp cloth and a steam iron.
• Plasti-tak is a helpful product for planning composition before attaching prints. It can be activated by stretching as taffy candy is stretched. You can use it under a print to hold it in place until you are satisfied with placement. When you remove it, it does not leave a spot or destroy the print, and it can be used repeatedly.
• A dampened paper towel must not be too wet when you are using it with a brayer over a glued print made from thin paper. Too much dampness can disintegrate the print.
• You must remove excess glue and air bubbles from prints you have glued. Roll with a brayer over a dampened paper towel from the center of the design out to each of the four corners; do not roll back and forth.
• If you make a mistake and damage the color in working with your print, you can use colored pencils to fill in the damaged area.
• To prepare gold decoupage braid for gluing, and to seal in the gold color in one step, rub white glue on your thumb and index finger and run the braid through those fingers.
• To hasten drying time between coats of decorative painting, spray the wet paint with a fixative.
• Use a shading sponge to blend colors and give texture to a painted design.
• In gluing with Velverette Craft Glue, apply adhesive to both whatever you plan to attach and the surface to which you plan to attach it.
• When gluing a raised cutout to a surface, apply finish to the surface and the cutout separately before gluing. Let finish dry completely before gluing.
• Heavy cutouts glued to a surface should be weighted until the glue dries completely.
• To glue shells to a surface and to insure their staying glued, glue cotton to the back of the shell first, then glue the cotton-backed shell to the surface.
• Use very fine steel wool (#0000) for a fine finish on decoupaged objects. (Regular commercial steel wool will scratch the finish.)
• Let a finished piece of decoupage harden for several weeks before applying the final finishing coat of decoupage wax.
• Use only white decoupage wax, not yellow or brown, on decoupaged objects.

- A square of a man's old felt hat is the best polishing cloth for decoupage.
- To clean glass objects to be used for decoupage under glass, wash the glass with soap and water, not vinegar; vinegar might effect the color of the prints.
- Instant decoupage can be used on photographs.
- Put a collar of aluminum foil around an open jar of instant decoupage to keep the jar lid from sticking because of excess finish in your brush that you have wiped on the jar's edge.
- When applying coats of instant decoupage, put the brush in a plastic bag between applications so it will not dry or harden.
- "Petitfours" are tiny sponges good for applying instant decoupage, glue, or acrylic paint without leaving streak marks or brush strokes.
- Instant spray finish can be applied over instant decoupage on a decoupaged piece that might water-spot, or on one that must be cleaned by washing.
- Contoured cutouts in dimensional decoupage can be placed on fabric, felt, burlap, bark, and cork, as well as over a duplicate print.
- Designs on very thin paper can be used for dimensional decoupage if you seal the back of the paper with 3 misty coats of decoupage sealer before cutting the print.
- Decoupage scissors of good quality should never be shared with anyone (here you really must be selfish!) and should never be used to cut anything but paper.
- Eliminate a white area on the edge of a print after cutting it by coloring the area with a matching colored pencil.
- To apply silicone sealer to a small area in dimensional decoupage, squeeze out a small amount on a paper plate or a piece of aluminum foil and apply it to the cutout with a toothpick.
- If you cannot find silicone sealer for elevating cutouts in dimensional decoupage, you can glue down balsa wood or pieces of Styrofoam, but you will not be able to achieve the same amount of contouring as with the sealer.
- If you prefer not to cover a dimensional decoupage picture with glass, you can brush on coats of glass stain extender over the print or spray with coats of decoupage finish.
- To prevent paper from splitting when stretching it for repoussé, cover the back of the print first with several coats of instant decoupage.
- To determine the area to be stretched for repoussé, hold a print with the design against the window so that you can see the design through the paper. On the back of the print, pencil in the areas to be stretched.

Floral Arrangements

- Use a piece of dry florist oasis to display or arrange delicate, small dried flowers.
- A Polaroid film carrier makes a good frame for dried flowers.
- Never use Stickum next to silver as it will discolor the silver permanently. Use a plate as a liner between Stickum and the silver object.
- To wire plastic fruits and vegetables for an arrangement, heat an ice pick, make a hole in the plastic, and insert a plastic stem or wire. (Save all stems you cut away when you shorten stems on plastic flowers.)

Bottle Cutting

- "No deposit, no return" bottles are good for practicing bottle cutting.
- To prevent an explosion when cutting bottles, remove bottle caps or corks before heating bottles.
- When cutting a bottle do not cut over a label. If you wish to preserve the label, remove it with hot water and later glue it back on the cut bottle.

Miscellaneous

- Flemish flowers are made by dipping old plastic flowers into a mixture of one pint varnish, one pint turpentine, one pint mahogany stain, ½-teaspoon burnt umber oil paint, and ½-teaspoon black oil paint. The mixture can be stored and reused.
- Plastic flowers are given a porcelain finish when dipped in a mixture of one pint turpentine, one pint clear varnish, and ¼-pint high gloss white enamel. Store for later use.
- Too much dye or scent added to candles when making them will ruin them.
- The type of mold determines the pouring temperature for candle wax: 190 to 200 degrees for metal; 145 to 150 degrees for plastic and rubber; 145 degrees for cardboard; 170 degrees for glass.
- To prevent fabric cutouts from fraying, coat the front and back of the fabric with instant decoupage, let dry, and then cut.
- After you have glued brown paper over the back of a frame, go over the paper with a damp sponge. When the paper dries, it will shrink and tighten.

• To make it easy to string beads on metallic crochet thread, apply glue to the ends of the thread to stiffen it before beads are added.

• To get a lining pattern for a box or purse, use aluminum foil. It will bend and crease easily, especially over contoured areas.

• Before you discard magazines, cards, calendars, stationery, or gift wrapping paper, cut out material you might wish to use later in your craft projects. Store in a box or portfolio.

• Read directions on a label before using the product. Oftentimes products that are similar will have different directions.

• One of the best, easiest, and neatest ways to glue a variety of surfaces together is to use one of the spray adhesives. At the time this book was written, however, spray adhesives were found to be harmful to the user and were taken off the market. Substitutions—in most cases Velverette Craft Glue—were made throughout the book. If, at any time, however, the product is improved and placed back on the market, by all means use it. It makes gluing much simpler and a lot less messy.

Papier-Mâché

• Tear paper for papier-mâché projects; do not cut. The rough edges of torn paper strips make the patterns stand out and give an interesting texture when the surface is painted.

• Heavy-duty aluminum foil can be shaped as a mold for papier-mâché strips, commercial mâché, or Sculptamold.

• Commercial papier-mâché can be mixed, rolled out between two sheets of waxed paper, and cut into shapes and designs.

• For a smoother finish in papier-mâché, cover the object with gesso before applying any type of paint.

Drying Plant Materials

• Flowers intended for drying should be gathered at mid-day after the dew has dried.

• Since many wildflowers are becoming extinct, they should not be used for flower drying. Besides, wildflowers do not dry very well.

• Some flowers and weeds can be dried by hanging them upside down in a brown paper bag and letting them dry at house temperature.

• If you insert wire stems into heavy flowers before drying, the drying process will tighten the flowers to the wire stems.

• To keep delicate petals from flattening when you are drying "cluster" flowers (such as lilacs and snapdragons), place 3 cardboard dividers into a cardboard box lengthwise. Cut sawtoothed notches into the dividers about halfway down and suspend the flowers for drying by placing the stems in these sawtoothed grooves.

• Fresh flowers can be dried in silica gel, in sterilized sand, in kitty litter, or in a mixture of 1 part borax to 1 part cornmeal. Silica gel is best because it dries flowers quickly, and thus they retain much of their color.

• When the blue granules of silica gel have turned white or pink, they have absorbed their moisture capacity. Reactivate them by placing the granules in a 225-degree oven on a cookie sheet for 15 minutes. Turn off the heat and let them remain in the oven until the granules turn blue; then place them in an airtight jar.

• Foliage may be dried by crushing the ends of the stem with a hammer blow, then placing the stem in a jar filled with a solution of $\frac{1}{3}$ glycerin to $\frac{2}{3}$ water.

• Dried flowers will last longer and be less fragile if you secure the petals by applying a little glue to the center inside of the flower and to the outside calyx.

• If a dried flower petal falls off, you can glue it back on with white glue.

• Decoupage sealer sprayed over dried flowers gives them body and protects the delicate foliage.

• After weeds are completely dried, they can be sprayed any color.

Household Supplies

Many of the projects in this book require tools and aids in addition to those contained within your workbasket. These are materials that can be found in most households. Have on hand some newspaper, cardboard, sponges, plastic bags, a hand or electric saw, paper towels, soap, rags, cloth, needle and thread, facial tissue, and string.

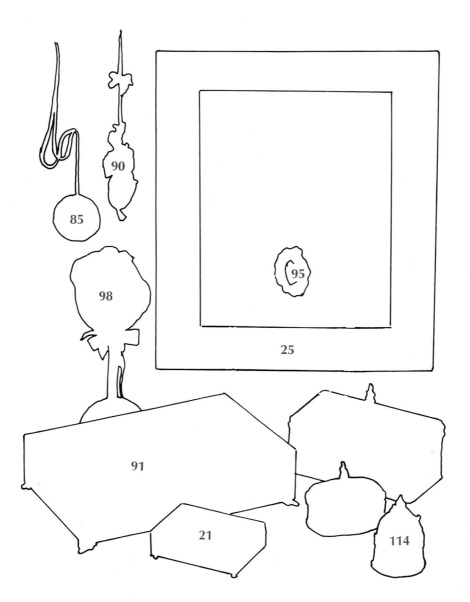

Details and instructions for projects shown may be found on page number indicated

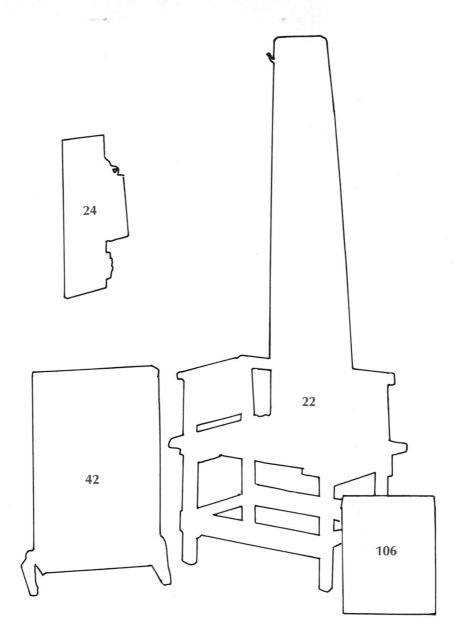

Details and instructions for projects shown may be found on page number indicated

Chapter
1

Home Furnishings and Decorations

Eggshell What-not Box
Hall Coat Rack and Bench
Kitchen Grater Wall Lamp
Frame Your Jewelry
Jigsaw Puzzle Table
Decoupaged Window Shade
Aluminum Can Floral Centerpiece
Sunburst Wall Hanging
Coffee Mug Recipe Holder
Salad Bowl Bird Feeder
Military Boot Lamp
Table Leg Lamp
Meat Grinder Lamp
Magazine Rack
Gold Leaf Candy Jar
Guest Towel Container
Owl Wall Decoration
Meat Grinder Wall Plaque
Three-Dimensional Picture under Phonograph Lid
Belted Wastepaper Basket

Eggshell What-not Box

(See completed project on page 16.)

Don't throw away the eggshells that usually go into your garbage pail. Crushed shells and a small wooden box in need of refinishing can become a very pretty what-not box for a living room table or a bedroom dresser top. This pearl-painted mosaic finish is so attractive that once you've learned how to do it, you'll want to use it on purses, jewelry boxes, mirrors, and picture frames.

Materials

wooden box with lid
wood putty
sandpaper: #220, 400, 600
acrylic paint in pastel color of your choice
eggshells (thoroughly cleaned and dried)
white glue
natural pearl paint
lacquer thinner
Treasure Sealer, spray or brush-on
instant spray finish, brush-on clear vinyl varnish,
**   or a clear lacquer finish**
Liquid Leaf in color of your choice (I used a gold
**   shade)**
new hardware (optional: to replace old
**   hardware, if any, and if not in good**
**   condition)**
Plasti-tak

Procedure

1. Inspect box. Remove hardware, if any, and fill holes with wood putty. Sand well inside and outside. Dry wipe with lint-free cloth.

2. Apply 1 coat of acrylic paint to outside box and lid, and inside lip edge of both. Let dry.

3. Put eggshells in a plastic bag and crush them by pounding the bag up and down against a table until the shells are the size of soap flakes.

4. Place the bottom half of the box upside down and apply a coat of white glue to the bottom. Take a handful of the crushed shells and sprinkle over the glued area. Let dry. (Best way to dry is to place box on a can so it won't stick to work surface and will dry evenly.) Tap slightly to remove excess flakes. If an area is uncovered, apply more glue and add more shell flakes. (Be careful not to get shells on the lip edge of the box, or on the ball feet.) When dry, turn the box and repeat the procedure until all sides of the box are covered. Let dry. Repeat procedure with top lid of box.

5. Apply 2 coats of natural pearl paint, following directions on the label. Apply a thin first coat. When dry, brush on a second heavier coat, brushing in the same direction. (*Optional:* For a true pearl look, apply the paint with a soft sponge and swirl in little circles.) Clean brushes thoroughly with lacquer thinner immediately after use.

6. Apply 3 misty coats of Treasure Sealer spray, or 2 coats of the brush-on Treasure Sealer, allowing drying time between coats. Let dry.

7. Apply at least 4 coats of spray finish, vinyl varnish, or lacquer to protect your finish, following directions on the label. Allow drying time between coats. Do not try to bury the flakes because the textured look is interesting. If you wish to smooth your finish, sand lightly and carefully after your protective coatings have dried thoroughly.

8. Paint the inside of the box and the lid with 1 coat of Liquid Leaf. If you are not satisfied with the coverage, apply a second coat when the first is dry. Let dry.

9. Apply 2 coats of Treasure Sealer over Liquid Leaf, allowing drying time between coats.

10. If the box lid is to be attached by hinges, place the top and the bottom of the box together; hold in position with Plasti-tak. Measure carefully to place hinges and mark screw holes with a pencil. Start holes for screws with an awl. Place the hinges, set in screws about halfway, and then go back and tighten screws. Remove Plasti-tak.

VARIATION: Line the box with fabric or wallpaper.

Hall Coat Rack and Bench

(See completed project on page 19.)

Two old washboards plus one old wooden ironing board equal a hall coat rack and bench that is extremely useful and quite attractive. Your guests will be amazed when you tell them what you used to make it.

Materials

2 washboards
wooden ironing board
scrap lumber (see "Procedure")
#220 sandpaper
wood putty (optional)
gesso
latex or acrylic paint in color of your choice
instant decoupage (Fun Podge, Mod Podge, Decollage)
leftover fabric with an interesting design
waxed paper or plastic sheeting
Plasti-tak
brayer
instant spray finish
clothing hooks (optional)
foam rubber: size of seat (optional)

Procedure

1. Remove metal (or glass on very old washboards) panels from washboards. Saw off legs on both sides 2 inches below the bottom edge of the wooden facings. Sand well. Put all pieces aside.

2. Remove leg supports from wooden ironing board.

3. Cut the following pieces from scrap lumber, or have lumberyard do this for you, and sand edges.

   1 seat: 15 inches × 24 inches × 1 inch
   2 bottom support strips: 2½ inches × 21 inches × 1 inch
   1 ironing board support strip (seat level): 4 inches × 17 inches × 1 inch
   1 ironing board support strip (washboard level): 1 inch × 21 inches × 1 inch
   1 back under-seat support strip: 3 inches × 21 inches × ¼ inch
   2 side under-seat support strips: 2 inches × 10¾ inches × 1 inch

4. Assemble. Nail washboard legs to seat with base supports in between. Line up washboard tops with bottoms and secure to seat. Nail on back supports. Nail and bolt ironing board in place.

5. *Optional:* Fill in any bad areas with wood putty, if necessary. Sand well.

6. Apply a coat of gesso over the entire unit and let dry, then sand well. Repeat.

7. Apply 3 coats of latex or acrylic paint, allowing adequate drying time between coats.

8. Brush 1 coat of instant decoupage over the entire unit. Allow to dry completely.

9. Brush 1 coat of instant decoupage over the fabric, keeping waxed paper or plastic sheeting underneath. Lift the fabric before it dries so it does not stick to the waxed paper. When dry, turn the fabric and repeat the procedure on the other side so your material will cut easily and will not ravel. Let dry.

10. Cut out designs from your fabric and work out the composition on the face of the ironing board, and on the wooden facings of the washboards, which will be the sides of the unit. Use Plasti-tak to hold the cutouts in place until you are satisfied with the arrangement.

11. Lift off the designs, one at a time, removing the Plasti-tak and leaving a tiny pencil mark where they are to be glued. Glue each one separately with instant decoupage. Roll out excess glue and air bubbles with a brayer over a dampened paper towel.

12. Brush 2 additional coats of instant decoupage over the fabric-covered areas, allowing drying time between coats.

13. Apply 2 misty coats of instant spray finish over the unit, allowing adequate drying time between coats.

14. *Optional:* Paint clothing hooks in desired color; let dry. Attach to chair back.

15. *Optional:* Cover foam rubber with matching fabric to make a cushion for the seat.

VARIATION: Proceed through step 5, then stain in color of your choice.

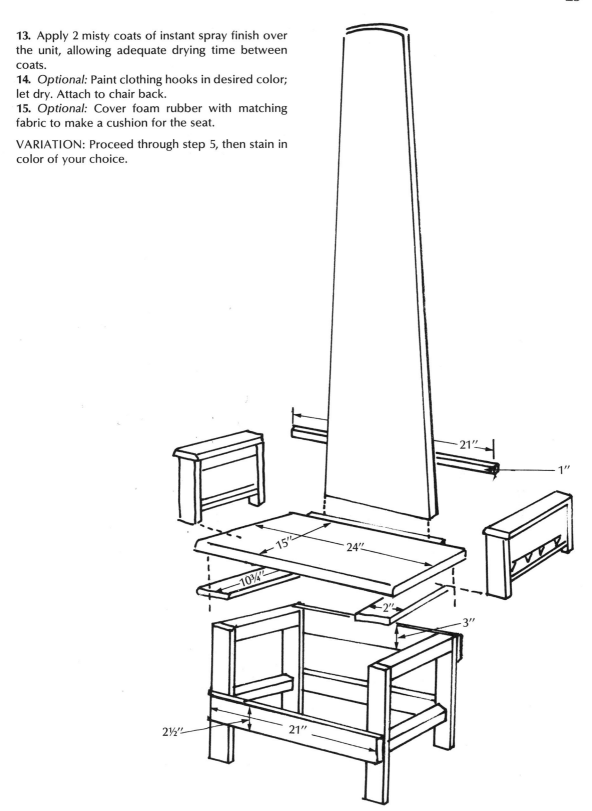

metal polish or metal finish, such as Lustre Wax,
  Rub 'n Buff, Liquid Copper (optional: to
  brighten or refinish old drawer pull)
kitchen grater with 4 sides
acrylic paint for grater in color of your choice
lamp fixture
scrap of leftover wallpaper: size of wall plaque
metal zip-off ring from soda can or saw-toothed
  metal picture hanger
spray finish or acrylic spray
2 yards burlap ribbon, ¾ inch wide, in color of
  your choice

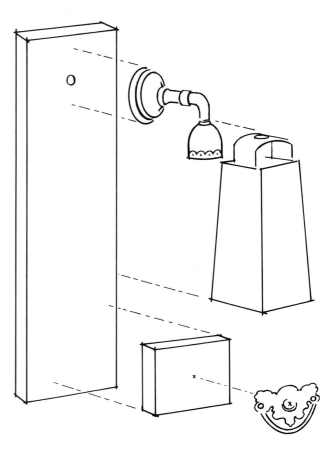

Kitchen Grater Wall Lamp

(See completed project on page 19.)
If the old-fashioned grater is an almost forgotten
utensil in your kitchen, don't throw it away. It
makes a fine kitchen wall light or night lamp for a
hall. I had an electrician assemble and wire my
lamp, and I suggest that you do the same. He will
have the materials and the tools, as well as the
electrical know-how.

Materials

scrap wood for wall plaque, 7½ inches × 19
  inches × ¾ inch (I used an old dresser
  front)
smaller piece of scrap wood, 3 inches × 6 inches
  × ¾ inch (I used side of old drawer)
dresser drawer pull
ammonia
#220 sandpaper
stain or paint of your choice (optional: for
  wood)
steel wool (optional: for staining)
gesso (optional: for painting)
water-base paint remover (optional: if you have
  to strip old paint)
vinegar

Procedure

1. Cut a piece of scrap wood to size (or remove front panel from old drawer). Cut the smaller wooden piece from scrap wood (or use side of drawer). Remove the drawer pull, if using drawer for wood. Wipe the wooden pieces with an ammonia and water solution to remove grease, if necessary. Sand all edges of the wood well.

If wood is stained, sand lightly, and renew finish with an application of matching stain, following directions on the label. Wipe off excess stain with a paper towel and allow to dry. Rub with steel wool.

If you wish to paint the wood, apply 1 coat gesso over old finish (either over stain or over old paint); allow to dry. Sand again. Apply 2 coats of any paint of your choice, allowing adequate drying time between coats.

If you wish to strip old paint—either to stain or repaint—use a water-base paint remover, following directions on the label. Work outdoors, if possible, and use rubber gloves.

2. Center and place the smaller wooden piece 1¼ inches from the 7½-inch bottom edge of the plaque. Nail it to the plaque from the back with several nails.

3. Wash the drawer pull, if it is old, with vinegar and water, and finish as you wish. You can polish it with a metal polish or finish it with a metal finish, or paint it in the color of your choice. When dry, nail or screw the drawer pull into the center of the wooden piece you nailed to the plaque.

4. Wash grater in a vinegar and water solution; dry well. Apply a thin coat of gesso; allow to dry. Apply 2 coats acrylic paint, inside and outside grater, allowing adequate drying time between coats. Trim rolled edge at grater bottom in a contrasting color, if you desire.

5. Assemble lamp, or have an electrician do it for you.

6. Use the plaque as a pattern to cut out a wallpaper backing for the lamp. Glue to the back of the plaque to prevent staining of the wall.

7. Center and nail a metal zip-off ring from a soda can or a saw-toothed picture hanger to the back of the plaque.

8. Apply 2 misty coats spray finish or acrylic spray to the front of the plaque, allowing drying time between coats.

9. Glue burlap ribbon around the edges of the plaque.

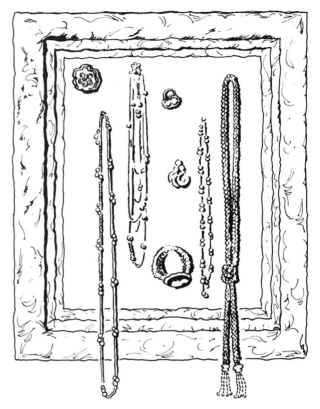

Frame Your Jewelry

(See completed project on page 16.)

Don't throw away old picture or mirror frames, even if they are in need of repair. There are many ways to re-style them and more than the obvious uses for them. I covered an old frame with foil, used a velveteen-covered board for the background, and inserted cup hooks. This is a good way to let your costume jewelry add decorative interest to your bedroom and to give you clutter-free drawers and tangle-free jewelry.

Materials

old frame
plaster of Paris or gesso (optional)
gold foil from florist plants or aluminum foil
white glue
antiquing glaze of your choice (optional)
spray finish
insulation board to fit inside frame

velveteen or felt to fit inside frame with 1-inch
    overlap on all edges
Velverette Craft Glue
masking tape
brown heavy-duty paper bag to fit back of frame
cup hooks

Procedure

1. Inspect the frame. Reglue any joints that seem
weak. If necessary, build up any damaged area with
gesso or plaster of Paris, following directions on the
label.
2. Cut strips of foil slightly longer than the frame
sides and twice the width. Wrinkle the foil; then,
straighten it out. Coat one side of the frame at a
time with white glue. Glue down a foil strip, wrapping the foil around to the back of the frame. Press
the foil into the crevices and press out bubbles.
Repeat the procedure, overlapping and mitering
corners, until the 4 sides are covered. Set aside to
dry.
3. *Optional:* Wipe antiquing glaze over the foil.
Wipe off excess with paper toweling, leaving some
antiquing in crevices of the foil. Let dry. If you
prefer a bright frame, omit this step.
4. Spray on 2 misty coats of spray finish, allowing
drying time between coats. Dry thoroughly.
5. Cut insulation board slightly smaller than needed
to fit the frame to allow for width of the fabric. Cut
fabric the size of the board plus a 1-inch overlap
on all sides. Check to be sure the fabric-covered
insulation board will fit the frame before gluing.
Glue fabric to board with Velverette Craft Glue.
Glue the back of the 1-inch fabric overlap, or the
back 1-inch margin of the insulation board (to permit easy removal of fabric if you decide to change
or refresh the fabric later). Mitre corners to eliminate bulk.
6. Insert the fabric-covered board into the back of
the frame. Hold in place with masking tape.
7. Cut a brown paper bag to cover the entire back
of the frame. Glue paper to all 4 sides of the frame
back.
8. Insert cup hooks into the board to hold your
jewelry according to your needs.

VARIATION 1: Use the frame for a cork memo
board in a girl's bedroom. Use push-pins instead
of cup hooks.

VARIATION 2: Repair frame with gesso and paint
it a bright color.

Jigsaw Puzzle Table
(See completed project on page 57.)

Have you ever finished one of the beautiful, circular
jigsaw puzzles and then regretted having to break
it up and put it away? Instead, you can keep it to
admire forever by converting it to a table top—the
base of which is a wooden barrel. Possible sources
for used wooden barrels are factories, carpenters
(who frequently purchase nails by the barrel), and
candy companies that ship their candies in barrels.

Materials

pine wood, ¾ inch thick (invest in good wood
    that will not warp; see "Procedure" for sizes
    of wood)
#220 sandpaper
wooden barrel (mine was 19 inches high)
gesso (optional)
latex or acrylic paint in color of your choice
    (pick out one of the least dominant colors in
    your puzzle, and one compatible with
    decor)
antiquing glaze

circular jigsaw puzzle (mine was 20½ inches in
  diameter)
cardboard to fit size of puzzle
waxed paper
instant decoupage (Fun Podge, Mod Podge,
  Decollage)
white glue
flexible decorative molding to fit table top
  circumference
marine varnish

Procedure

1. With a saw cut a circle from wood for the table
top the same diameter as the completed puzzle.
Cut a circle to fit the inside diameter of the top of
the barrel. (Each barrel must be measured for this
inside diameter—they are not all the same size.) Cut
a 15-inch-diameter circle for the base of the barrel.
Sand well.

2. Assemble. Center and nail the top inside-dia-
meter circle to the underside of the table-top circle.
Insert the nailed top into the barrel; the small circle
will fit inside the barrel and hold the top in place.
Nail the top to the barrel through the metal strip
on the barrel side. Center and nail the bottom (15-
inch) circle to the bottom of the barrel.

3. If the barrel is not in good condition, apply one
coat of gesso. Let dry.

4. Brush on 2 coats of latex or acrylic paint on all
outside areas of the barrel table, including the top.
Allow drying time between coats. Then let dry
overnight.

5. Apply antiquing glaze, according to directions
on the label. Wipe off excess with a textured paper
towel. Let dry overnight.

6. Work your puzzle on a circle of cardboard that
has the same diameter as the puzzle. Carefully slide
the finished puzzle from the cardboard onto waxed
paper for gluing. Keep the puzzle pieces tight.

7. Brush on 1 coat of instant decoupage over the
puzzle as a glue. Important: lift up the puzzle as it
begins to dry, so it will not stick to the paper. When
thoroughly dry, reverse the puzzle and place on
waxed paper. Brush a coat of instant decoupage on
the back. Let dry.

8. Glue the puzzle to the table top with white glue.
Weight the glued puzzle; check when weighted to
make sure you have not put the puzzle out of line.
(I turned my table upside down on a piece of plastic. The table itself acted as a weight on the top,

and it was easy to see if the puzzle was in line.) Dry
overnight.

9. When dry, apply several additional coats of instant decoupage to the table top, allowing drying
time between coats.

10. Nail on, or paste on, decorative molding
around the circumference edge of the table top.

11. To protect the paint and to prevent water
marking from spills, apply several coats of marine
varnish over the entire table, allowing adequate
drying time between coats.

VARIATION: Glue completed puzzle to canvas
board and hang on wall as a picture. Here you can
use a rectangular puzzle as well as a circular one.

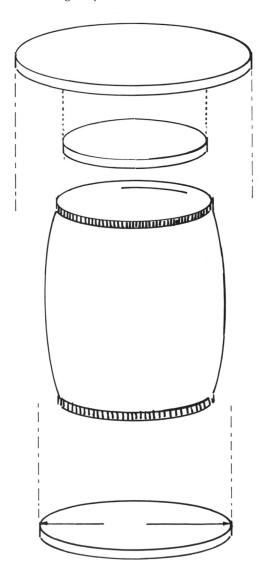

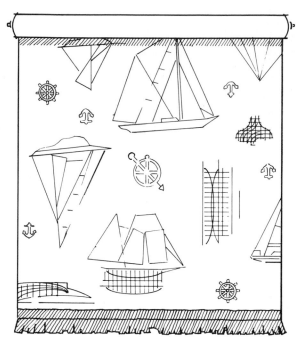

Decoupaged Window Shade

Don't throw away an old window shade roller and runner. With leftover fabric and instant decoupage, you can easily make a window shade to match your draperies or upholstery.

Materials

window shade roller
ammonia
leftover fabric in size to fit window (colors and pattern to complement room decor)
stain-repelling spray (optional)
waxed paper or plastic sheeting
instant decoupage (Fun Podge, Mod Podge, Decollage)
Velverette Craft Glue
window shade runner
decorative braid or fringe to match a color in fabric (optional)

tacks or heavy-duty staple gun
window shade pull (optional)

Procedure

1. Wipe roller with solution of ammonia and water to remove grease.
2. Cut out fabric (left over from draperies or upholstery) in size to fit window, but allowing for side hems plus an extra 2½ inches at bottom for shade runner.
3. Press fabric well. Spray it with a stain-repelling product (optional).
4. Lay out fabric on waxed paper or a plastic sheet. Brush instant decoupage on front of fabric until completely saturated; lift up fabric as it dries so it won't adhere to the paper or plastic. When completely dry, repeat on the other side.
5. Turn underside edges of the fabric (to fit window shade roller) and glue neat side hems with instant decoupage. Turn under a 2-inch channel for the shade runner at bottom of fabric; glue the edges of the hem to the fabric back with Velverette Craft Glue. (Remember to leave the channel open; that is, glue only the hem edges. You may prefer to stitch this channel.) Insert shade runner when the channel hem is dry, or stitched.
6. *Optional:* Glue on a decorative braid or fringe at the bottom of the shade.
7. Attach shade to the roller with tacks or a heavy-duty staple gun.
8. *Optional:* Attach a shade pull to center of shade bottom.

VARIATION 1: Following same procedure, substitute an attractive linen towel for leftover fabric and make a shade for a small window, such as in the kitchen or bathroom.

VARIATION 2: You may prefer to appliqué fabric cutouts to an old window shade. The method is quite similar to the preceding one.

Materials

old window shade in good working order
ammonia
instant decoupage (Fun Podge, Mod Podge, Decollage)
leftover fabric with an interesting design
waxed paper or plastic sheeting
Plasti-tak
fringe or braid trimming (optional)

Procedure

1. Wash and dry shade in a solution of soap, water, and ammonia. Dry well.

2. Brush a coat of instant decoupage over the front of the shade. Let dry.

3. Press fabric. Place on waxed paper or plastic sheeting. Brush a coat of instant decoupage on one side; lift the fabric as it dries, so it will not stick to the paper or plastic. When thoroughly dry, turn fabric over and repeat.

4. Cut out fabric designs to be attached to the shade. Plan your composition; hold the cutouts in place with Plasti-tak until you are satisfied with the arrangement.

5. Lift off the cutout pieces, one at a time, removing the Plasti-tak and leaving a tiny pencil mark where they are to be placed. Glue each one separately with instant decoupage. Roll out excess glue and air bubbles with a brayer over a dampened paper towel. Let dry.

6. *Optional:* Glue on braid or fringe trim to the edge of the shade with instant decoupage.

Aluminum Can Floral Centerpiece

The day before yesterday (or could it have been the day before that?) I was the mother of three lively teenagers. At the time I learned that the greatest throwaway in my home with teenagers is the soda pop can. It always broke my don't-throw-it-away heart to toss out by the score those empty containers. Today our soda pop comes in aluminum cans, which are a brand new and delightful craft medium. Aluminum cans can be cut with ordinary scissors, will fold flat into easily stored aluminum sheets, and can produce the most attractive flowers and foliage.

So don't throw away your aluminum soda pop cans. Instead, turn them into flowers and combine them, if you wish, with a live plant and an old rusty tea kettle to make one of the prettiest arrangements that could grace a table.

The following directions are for making one daisy with three leaves. When I combine the daisies with a live plant, I omit the aluminum leaves to give the arrangement a more realistic look. I also provide directions for restoring a rusty tea kettle in case you are lucky enough to have one and would like to make an arrangement similar to mine.

Materials

3 soft aluminum cans (non-citrus soda pop cans without seams; cans with seams are made of tin, not aluminum)

old-fashioned can opener (this type only)

sharp household scissors (not workbasket scissors—cutting aluminum dulls them)

shirt cardboard

compass (optional)

dry ball point pen

small piece Styrofoam

awl or ice pick

1 piece #16 wire

1 piece #22 (fine) wire

Stickum

gesso

acrylic or latex base paint: white, yellow, and green

green florist tape

semi-gloss spray finish

Procedure

1. Wash cans thoroughly. Put on rubber gloves.

2. With can opener puncture a hole in the side of the can near the top. Cut away the top with the opener; cut the last inch away with scissors.

3. With scissors cut down the side of the can and around the bottom. Trim away all uneven edges, spread out, and flatten. Repeat the procedure on the remaining 2 cans.

4. Using a compass or discs in appropriate sizes, draw on cardboard one 3½-inch circle, one 3-inch circle, one 1½-inch circle, and one 1¼-inch circle; also draw 3 leaves and a butterfly. See *Diagram A*. (If you plan to insert the daisy in fresh greens, you may omit the leaves. The butterfly, too, is optional.) Cut out the cardboard patterns with scissors. With a dry ball point pen (a pen that has gone dry will make a good mark without leaving an ink stain), trace the cardboard designs onto the aluminum sheets.

5. Place the aluminum sheets over a piece of Styrofoam to protect your work area. Use an awl, an ice pick, or the compass point to punch 2 holes in the center area of each of the three larger circles (3½, 3, and 1½ inches). Punch 1 hole in the center of the smallest circle (1¼ inches). These holes will be used later in assembling the flower.

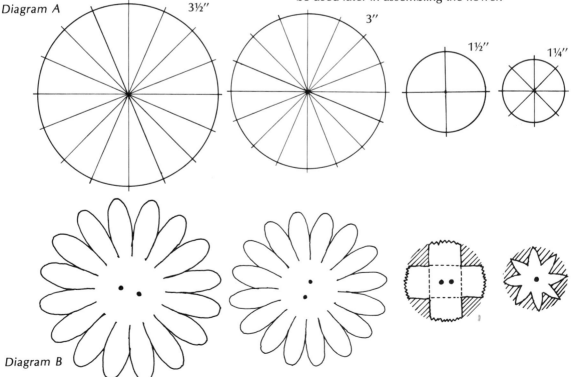

Diagram A   3½"   3"   1½"   1¼"

Diagram B

6. With the dry ball point pen, divide the two larger circles (3½ and 3 inches) in half, then into quarters, eighths, and sixteenths. (These 16 pie-shaped wedges will become your flower petals.) With your pen divide the 1½-inch circle into 4 quarters. Divide the 1¼-inch circle into 8 sections.

7. Cut out all circles, leaves, and the butterfly. Cut the 1½-inch circle into a surfer's cross by cutting away the shaded areas and fringe-cutting the ends as shown. See *Diagram B.* Cut the 1¼-inch circle into a star shape by cutting away the shaded areas. See *Diagram B.* Cut the 3½- and 3-inch circles into 16 petal-shaped sections by cutting on the lines toward the center of the circle (being careful not to cut into the assembly holes you made earlier). Cut the petal tips in a rounded daisy shape.

8. Shape the petals of these 2 larger circles by bending slightly lengthwise over the tip of an open pair of scissors. See *Diagram C.* (Long-nosed pliers are helpful if you have difficulty doing this with scissors.)

9. Take the fringed 1½-inch circle, and bend it into a cup shape (daisy stamen); put it on top of the 3-inch circle. Place the 3½-inch circle underneath these two, staggering the petals as you assemble them. See *Diagram D.*

10. Bend the #16 wire into an upside-down U loop. Insert from the top through the holes in the stamen circle, through the holes in the 2 petal circles. Hold both ends of wire together without twisting and insert through the single hole of the 1¼-inch calyx circle. Before tightening with a piece of fine #22 wire, put a small piece of Stickum between the bottom petal and the calyx. Tighten the entire flower unit and twist the #22 wire tightly around the #16 wire at the base of the calyx. Let the 4 ends of the wires dangle. (See *Diagram D.*)

11. Shape a piece of Stickum into a ball in your hand. Insert it into the fringed stamen cup. Pinch the ends of the cup to hold it securely.

Diagram C

12. Paint all petals, leaves, and butterfly (including Stickum stamen) with 1 coat gesso. Allow gesso to dry. If you are making leaves and the butterfly, make indentations to vein the leaves, and draw the butterfly detail with an awl or ice pick while the gesso is still wet.

13. Paint the daisy petals with white acrylic paint. Paint the stamen center yellow. Paint the calyx and leaves green. Paint the butterfly as you wish. (There are many ways to paint the daisy: spraying, dipping, hand painting. Although it takes more time and care, I prefer the hand-painting method with a gesso undercoat. The flowers take on a textured

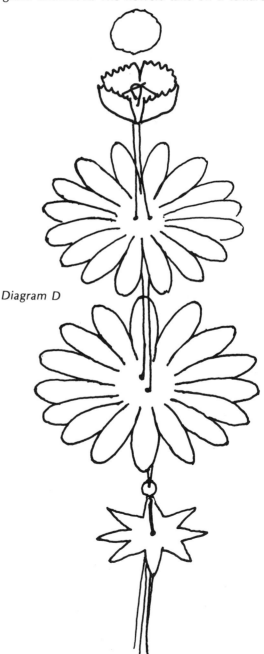

Diagram D

look that makes them appear real, and the paint clings better.) If you are not satisfied with coverage, paint a second coat. Allow to dry.

14. Starting under the calyx, tape the wire of the daisy with green florist tape, stretching and pulling the tape as you twist. (Florist tape is not sticky until stretched.) Twist the tape, not the wires. Add leaves, staggering their position as you tape.

15. Spray a coat of semi-gloss finish on the daisy. Allow to dry.

16. *Optional:* Make several daisies. Tuck them into a plant that is in an interesting container, such as the tea kettle described here. (See completed project in photograph facing page 70.)

Materials

rusted tea kettle
vinegar
turpentine or mineral spirits
wire brush, steel wool, or sandpaper
Rustoleum (optional)
gesso
acrylic or latex base paint
semi-gloss spray finish

Procedure

1. Wash the kettle with vinegar, soap, and water to remove grease.

2. Wash with turpentine or mineral spirits to remove lacquer.

3. Remove rust with a wire brush, steel wool, or sandpaper. If rust persists, apply Rustoleum, following directions on the can.

4. Apply 1 coat of gesso over the entire kettle.

5. Apply 2 coats of acrylic paint, allowing adequate drying time between coats (I used the same yellow as my daisy centers). Dry thoroughly.

6. Spray with 1 coat of semi-gloss finish.

Sunburst Wall Hanging

(See completed project on page 55.)

Miles, the art director of our TV show, *All About Crafts,* came up with many creative ideas in the course of taping the show, but his final project had special meaning. It was a gold sunburst wall hanging made from all the discarded cassette tins of our TV tapes and camera film containers, and Miles gave it to me.

If there are no 16 mm. film cans in your life, you can use the tops from any cans with wide lids, such as candy, cookie, nut, or popcorn tins, or tops from ½-gallon ice cream cans. You can make the center area of the sunburst from the containers used to hold film for 35 mm. slide cameras. The sunburst can be any size you wish simply by increasing or decreasing the size of your base circle and the number of tops you use. And you can spray it to match whatever color suits your decor.

These are the directions based upon the way Miles made mine. Vary the directions to suit the size and look you desire.

Materials

Masonite for the circular base, 22 inches diameter
#220 sandpaper
tin snips
large circular can top for center, approximately 8 inches diameter (possibly a cookie can top or top of an anti-freeze can)
12 bottoms from 35 mm. camera film containers, 19 tops from 35 mm. camera film containers, 34 can tops, approximately 8 inches in diameter, 22 for inside rim and 12 for outside rim (could be 16 mm. movie film containers or ½-gallon ice cream containers)
epoxy glue
gold leaf spray or acrylic spray paint in color of your choice
crystal clear glaze (optional)
black antiquing spray (optional)
large saw-toothed metal picture hanger

Procedure

1. Draw a 22-inch circle on Masonite; cut out with saw or have someone do this for you. Sand edges well. Put on cotton gloves.

2. With tin snips cut side edges of the 8-inch can top into triangular points, about 1 inch apart. With flat side down, bend the pointed edge backward and away from you, like a petal, over the edge of an open pair of scissors. Glue in center of Masonite circle with flat side against Masonite.

3. Flatten down the bottoms of 12 camera film cans (35 mm.) by stepping on them as children step on tin cans. Assemble them like petals tucked around and under the outside edges of the 8-inch circle. Glue in place.

4. Evenly fill the 8-inch tin circle with the tops of 19 camera film cans. Glue in place.

5. Fold the ice cream or movie film tops in half, edges facing and slightly open. Place 22 tops around the center design in a sunburst pattern. Place 12 tops around the outside rim of the Masonite circle. Glue in place. Allow to dry thoroughly before painting.

6. Spray entire wall hanging with several misty coats of gold leaf spray, allowing adequate drying time between coats.

7. If you wish the plaque to stay shiny, spray with crystal clear glaze. If you like an antiqued effect, spray with a black antiquing spray and wipe off excess with a paper towel. If you have not sprayed it with crystal clear glaze, exposure to the air will antique the gold naturally after a time. If the gold eventually becomes discolored, you can always respray.

8. Attach picture hanger to the back.

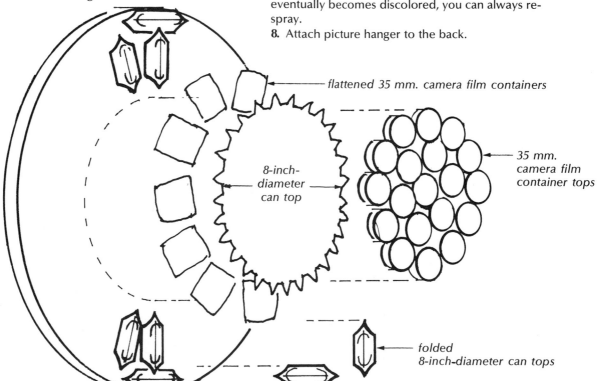

flattened 35 mm. camera film containers

35 mm. camera film container tops

8-inch-diameter can top

folded 8-inch-diameter can tops

Coffee Mug Recipe Holder

Procedure

1. If the mug is cracked, apply a coat of gesso over entire mug, inside and outside.
2. Spray outside of mug with several misty coats of spray paint. Allow to dry thoroughly between coats. (This step should be omitted if you want to retain the original appearance of the mug.)
3. Insert Styrofoam in mug and cover with moss.
4. Insert plastic vegetables into moss-covered Styrofoam. Insert the bee on a wire into the arrangement. Place a plastic plant cardholder into the arrangement.
5. Apply 2 misty coats of spray finish or acrylic spray over mug. Allow to dry completely between coats.
6. Attach recipe card to the plastic cardholder.

(See completed project on page 30.)

If you've cracked or damaged a coffee mug, don't throw it away. With a minimum of effort you can turn it into a recipe card holder. This is a good way, too, to use the only mug left from a set or a single mug given as a gift.

I particularly like this idea because it has so many uses. It makes reading a recipe and cooking at the same time a breeze. It's a marvelous hostess gift. It's a wonderful gift for a bride's kitchen shower, especially if you make it personal by writing one of your favorite recipes on a recipe card. Depending on the way you decorate it, you can use it in a nursery for instructions for the baby sitter, or on a teenager's bureau to list the week's activities and assignments.

Materials

coffee mug
gesso (optional)
spray paint in color of your choice (optional)
Styrofoam to fit inside mug
moss
miniature plastic vegetables on stems or wires
artificial bee
wire
plastic plant cardholder (saved from florist's plants or flowers)
spray finish or acrylic spray
recipe card

Salad Bowl Bird Feeder

(See completed project on page 173.)

Two somewhat tired salad bowls of different sizes and a wooden dowel stick make a squirrel-proof, waterproof bird feeder. Because the top is rounded, the squirrels have difficulty with footing. The seed, held in the smaller upright salad bowl at the bottom, is protected and kept dry. Birds don't like painted feeders, so all you have to do is to cut a few dowels, drill a few holes, and put it together.

Materials

1 12-inch dowel, ⅝-inch diameter
4 2-inch pieces of dowel, ¼-inch diameter
#220 sandpaper
2 salad bowls, 1 slightly larger than the other (my bowls had 9-inch and 10½-inch diameters)
drill (if you don't own one, borrow a friend's)
1½ yards leather thong

Procedure

1. Cut dowels to size; sand edges.
2. Drill holes in the centers of the 2 salad bowls that are large enough for your ⅝-inch-diameter dowel to fit tightly in; check fit.
3. Drill ¼-inch-diameter holes in the 12-inch dowel: 1 inch from the top, 2¾ inches from the top, and 2 inches from the bottom. Insert a small dowel through the bottom hole and another through the hole 2¾ inches from the top. Do not put a dowel through the very top hole.
4. Insert the larger salad bowl on top of the large dowel upside down. Push it down until it sits on the top small dowel. Mark line with a pencil where the salad bowl and larger dowel meet at the top. Remove the salad bowl and drill a ¼-inch-diameter hole for another small dowel, above the pencil line, at a right angle to the hole previously drilled, moving up far enough to allow for the ¼-inch-width of the small dowel. (Drilling the holes at right angles will eliminate the risk of weakening and splitting the dowel.)
5. Insert the smaller salad bowl on the bottom of the large dowel right side up. Push it up until it touches the small dowel at the bottom. Mark line with a pencil where the salad bowl and larger dowel meet at the bottom. Remove the salad bowl and drill a ¼-inch-diameter hole for another small dowel, below the pencil line, at a right angle to the hole previously drilled, moving down far enough to allow for the ¼-inch-width of the small dowel.
6. Assemble feeder. Put small bowl back in position and secure it at the bottom with small dowel. Put larger bowl back on the top of dowel, upside down, and secure it at the top with small dowel. Insert leather thong through top hole for hanging.

7. Insert an end of leather thong for hanging the feeder through the top hole in the large dowel. Draw the ends together and knot in a double knot at the top.

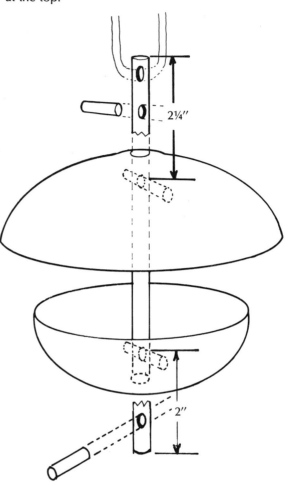

Military Boot Lamp

(See completed project on page 7.)

Turn an old military boot into something pretty and peaceful, instead of throwing it away. If it is painted, wired with a light fixture, and decorated with flowers, the boot can become a lamp for a child's room.

This lamp is really not difficult to attach. So, while I usually recommend that your local electrician do the job, I think you might try this one on your own if you know how to connect and disconnect the wires and the plug.

Materials

old military boot
vinegar (optional)
adhesive tape (optional)
scrap lumber for base board (my board is 13 inches × 7½ inches, but measurement depends on boot size; leave at least a 1-inch border around boot sole)
#220 sandpaper
gesso
acrylic paint in colors of your choice (I used pink for the boot and white for the base)

lamp fixture (an old one, or purchase at hardware store or dime store)
drill
instant decoupage (Fun Podge, Mod Podge, Decollage)
bolt (lamp fixture may come with one; if not, buy separately)
felt to fit bottom of base board
white glue
4 decorative hardware feet or upholstery tacks
2 yards ribbon trim
pieces of Styrofoam to fit inside boot
sprigs of artificial flowers and greens
shoe lace in color to match boot
ceramic pixie or small stuffed toy
lampshade of your choice (I made a shingled roof)

Procedure

1. Remove old shoe laces from boot. If boot is dirty, wash with a vinegar and water solution. Dry thoroughly. If the boot is split or badly worn, tape the problem area. (I used adhesive tape to cover a hole in the side of my boot.)

2. Cut base board to size; sand edges. Apply 2 coats of gesso to the board and the boot, allowing drying time between coats.

3. Apply 2 coats of acrylic paint to the boot, allowing drying time between coats.

4. Disconnect the wire from the plug of the light fixture. When boot is thoroughly dry, center it on board, leaving a 1-inch border around it, to determine where you wish to drill the holes for wiring. Insert the light fixture from the top down into boot; the wire will go through the sole of boot, through the base board, and out the bottom of board. Mark the position for these holes. Remove the light fixture and set aside. Drill a hole through the bottom of the boot and through the board.

5. Apply 2 coats of instant decoupage to the boot to prevent the paint from chipping; allow adequate drying time between coats.

6. Apply 2 coats of acrylic paint in the color of your choice to the board; allow to dry thoroughly.

7. Apply 2 coats of instant decoupage to the board.

8. When the board is thoroughly dry, assemble the lamp. Place the fixture in the boot through the holes prepared for it. Bolt the fixture in place at the bottom of the board. Connect the plug and the wires.

9. Glue felt, cut to fit, to the bottom of the board. Cut away felt around the light fixture opening. Because of the protruding wire at the base of the board, attach decorative feet or upholstery tacks at each of the corners to elevate the board.

10. Glue ribbon trim around edges of board.

11. Pull flap of boot down, as shown in diagram. Wedge pieces of Styrofoam inside the boot on each side of the lamp fixture. Insert sprigs of artificial flowers and greens into the Styrofoam.

12. Lace boot with a clean shoe lace, if you wish. Glue a pixie or stuffed toy to boot front or insert in between flowers in boot.

13. Attach a lampshade of your choice. The means of securing lampshade to bulb will depend on the kind of lampshade you use.

VARIATION 1: Make a lamp for a horseback riding fan from a riding boot. Since riding boots are usually kept clean and sparkling, finishing of the boot is seldom necessary. Paint or stain the board in the color of your choice.

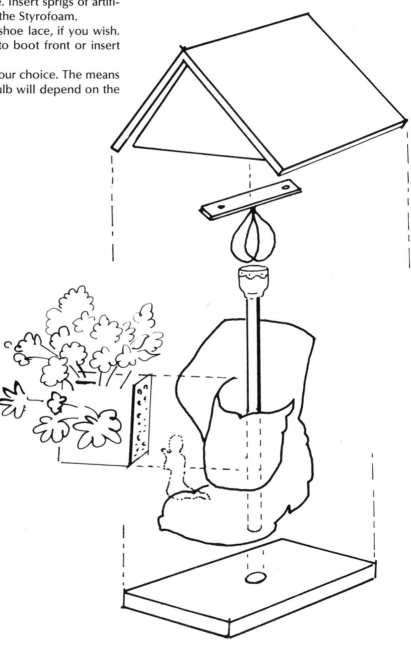

Table Leg Lamp

(See completed project on page 57.)

House sales, which are common events in many communities, offer some remarkable finds. But few people realize that among the unsold, discarded items there often are unexpected treasures. I once rescued an abandoned table with one broken leg, removed the good legs, and with the help of a gold leafing kit and an electrician, made a pair of attractive lamps for my living room. Look for tables with carved or unusual-shaped legs at house and garage sales.

Materials

wooden table leg
block of wood (if necessary; my table legs were too narrow at the bottom to stand upright without support, so I used 5- × 5- × 4-inch blocks)
#220 sandpaper
drill (optional)
lamp fixture (or have an electrician supply and wire)
wood putty (optional)
gesso
acrylic paint in color of your choice
gold leaf adhesive (a regular adhesive will dry too quickly)*
packet of gold metal leaf*
sable hobby brush (label and use only for gold leaf work)*
old nylon stocking
gold leaf sealer*
decoupage braid to go around the lamp base (select according to decor)
white glue
decoupage sealer
gold leaf antiquing glaze (optional)
lamp shade of your choice

These materials are available together in a gold leafing kit, or they may be purchased separately.

Procedure

1. Check the table leg and determine where to saw off; saw, and sand raw edges.
2. Have a carpenter perform this step if you don't own a drill. If the table leg is solid wood, drill vertically through the center of the leg for wiring (some table legs are hollow in the center). Drill a hole vertically through the center of the wooden block, if you plan to use it for a support. Drill another hole in one side of the wooden block near the bottom, horizontally, halfway across the block to meet the center hole you have already drilled. This will permit your wiring to go through the center of the lamp and come out at a side near the bottom.
3. Plan to construct your lamp completely before you do any decorative work. Take the wooden pieces to an electrician and select the type fixture you wish to use. My electrician bolted the small metal lamp bases to the wooden base pieces, attached the wooden table leg on top of the metal base, and put the post and sockets and finial on top of the table leg.
4. Sand all wood well.
5. *Optional:* Fill any deep surface dents in the table leg with wood putty. Sand and wipe again.
6. Apply 1 coat of gesso to the table leg and wooden block to seal the wood and prevent chipping. Sand again.
7. Apply 1 coat of acrylic paint in the color of your choice. (Gold leaf experts like a colored undercoating to show through the leaf.) Allow to dry completely.

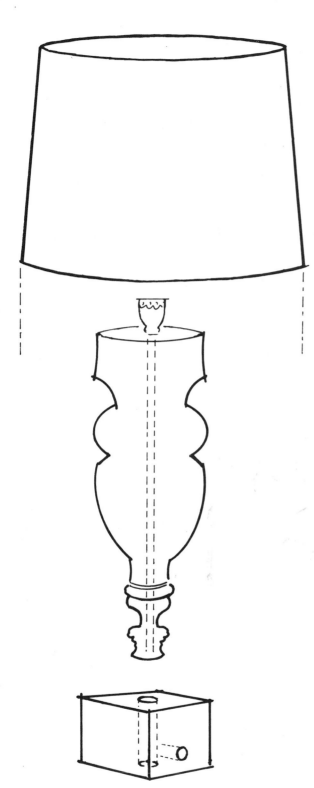

8. Brush gold leaf adhesive lightly but thoroughly on a section of the table leg. Do not apply adhesive to an area larger than you can foresee finishing at one sitting. Leafing will not adhere to any part of the surface not covered by adhesive. Wait 30 to 45 minutes, or until the adhesive turns clear. Test the proper adhesive consistency by pressing your knuckle against the surface. If you feel a slight clicking pull, the adhesive is ready for gold leafing. (Note: Work in a room where there's not much traffic; a breeze will cause gold leaf particles to fly.)

9. Apply the gold leaf to the area precoated with the adhesive; overlap slightly pieces of gold leaf. Since leaf tears when covering contoured surfaces, apply smaller pieces of leaf to those areas. Press leaf into place with the paper that separates the pieces of leaf in your packet, and lightly brush the leaf into crevices with the tip of a sable hobby brush. (Since I like cracks in gold leaf, I cut my gold leaf packet into 4 equal sections and do all my gold leafing with smaller pieces of leaf. If you do this, be sure to stack all pieces in the same direction, or you will reverse the leaf.) Repeat application of gold leaf adhesive and gold leaf to entire table leg.

10. Allow the gold leaf to set for several hours. Use your clean, dry sable brush to smooth out the leaf with a patting or tapping motion of the brush and with smooth, even strokes. Remove the seams where a piece of leaf overlaps another by brushing lightly in a back and forth motion.

11. Burnish the leaf by rubbing a nylon stocking lightly along the surface to remove gold flakes.

12. Brush on 2 light coats of gold leaf sealer to protect the leaf from tarnishing.

13. Glue decoupage braid on the top and bottom side edges of the wooden base block. Seal braid with 3 misty coats of decoupage sealer.

14. *Optional:* Apply gold leaf antiquing glaze over the entire lamp, according to directions on the label. Wipe off excess with a paper towel and rub the remainder down into the leaf to achieve an aged look. Omit rubbing down if you like a bright look.

15. Brush on 2 coats of gold leaf sealer.

16. Attach the lamp shade of your choice.

VARIATION: For a silver lamp, follow the same procedure with silver leaf products. Dip decoupage braid into decoupage thinner to remove the gold finish and turn the braid silver.

Meat Grinder Lamp

(See completed project in photograph facing page 1.)

I've said it before, but it bears repeating: don't throw away an old-fashioned meat grinder. Combined with an old cheese board and an empty apple basket, it makes an unusual lamp.

If you plan to do your own electrical work on this lamp (not recommended unless you know how), do the necessary drilling for the fixture first. If an electrician will complete the lamp, do all the major work first and then take it to him to be drilled and fitted. Your final decorative accents can be added after the electrician's work is done.

Materials

meat grinder
ammonia
wire brush, steel wool, or sandpaper
Rustoleum (optional)
piece of wood, 4 inches × 6 inches × ¾ inch
lamp fixture (purchase at a hardware store or have an electrician install)
apple basket, 6½ inches deep and 9 inches diameter
#220 sandpaper
gesso
cheese or bread board, approximately 9 inches × 15 inches
acrylic paint in 2 colors of your choice
spray finish or acrylic spray

wooden block to fit inside meat grinder opening
white glue
felt to fit cheese board base
screw or bolt for lamp fixture
2 yards ball fringe
bird's nest (found in craft stores)
several brads or heavy-duty stapler
Styrofoam to fit inside bird's nest
Stickum
moss to cover Styrofoam
hairpin or U-pin
artificial flowers
3 plastic jelly beans
sprig of artificial greens
artificial bird (found in craft stores)

Procedure

1. Wash the meat grinder thoroughly with ammonia and soapy water. Remove rust, if any, with a wire brush, steel wool, or sandpaper. If rust persists, apply Rustoleum, following directions on the can.
2. Wipe all wooden pieces with a rag dampened in an ammonia and water solution to remove all traces of grease. Sand well.
3. Center and drill a hole for the lamp fixture in the piece of wood, about 2 inches in from one of the 4-inch edges. Make sure the fixture can fit snugly into hole. Drill a hole of the same diameter in apple basket for fixture.
4. Apply 2 coats of gesso to the cheese board, the piece of wood, and the meat grinder, allowing drying time between coats. Sand. Apply 2 coats of acrylic paint in the colors of your choice to these same objects; allow drying time between coats.
5. Apply 2 coats of acrylic paint to the apple basket, inside and outside (a gesso base coat is not necessary here). (I painted the cheese board, piece of wood, apple basket, and meat grinder handle white. I painted the meat grinder and the decorative edge of the cheese board yellow.)
6. Apply 3 misty coats of spray finish or acrylic spray to each of the objects you painted; allow to dry completely between each coat.
7. Into the meat grinder opening, insert the wooden block you prepared for this purpose. Make sure it fits snugly into the grinder opening; otherwise, the grinder will tip when inverted and placed on the cheese board.

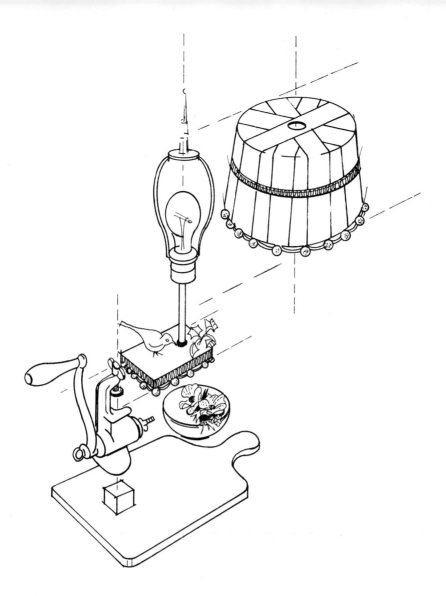

8. Turn the grinder upside down, with the opening facing the cheese board. Center the grinder 1½ inches in from the 9-inch straight edge of the board; attach by gluing the cheese board to the wooden block in the grinder opening. When glue is dry, reinforce by nailing in several places from the back of the cheese board through the wooden block.

9. Cut a piece of felt the size and shape of the cheese board and glue to the back.

10. Wipe the drilled hole in the 4- × 6-inch piece of wood with glue. Insert lamp fixture into hole; this should fit tightly. Attach a screw or bolt underneath to hold the lamp fixture securely in place.

11. Spray ball fringe with spray finish or acrylic spray. Allow to dry. Glue ball fringe around the 4 edges of the piece of wood, and around the bottom edge of the apple basket. Trim off the loops and

fringe balls from the remaining braid and glue braid around the center support strip of the apple basket.

12. Attach the undrilled end of wooden piece to grinder by fastening down grinder screw. (At this point the grinder screw will be upside down.)

13. Attach the apple basket shade to the lamp fixture through the hole drilled in the basket.

14. Attach the bird's nest to the cheese board with brads or a heavy-duty stapler. Cut Styrofoam to fit inside the nest and insert, attaching with a small piece of Stickum. Cover the Styrofoam with moss, secured with hairpin, wire or a U-pin. Insert artificial flowers (I used daffodils) into moss-covered Styrofoam in the nest; attach plastic jelly beans (for eggs) with Stickum or glue.

15. Wire the sprig of artificial greens to the base of the fixture. Glue the bird to the piece of wood, placing him on a few small twigs if you wish.

Magazine Rack

(See completed project on page 19.)

You can provide extra storage space for magazines by assembling a handsome magazine rack out of an old washboard and scrap lumber from old crates. Ask the supermarket manager to save you blueberry or melon crates; they have the best lumber for this purpose.

Materials

scrap lumber from wooden crates for rack facings, sides, and feet (see "Procedure")
large washboard, approximately 23 inches × 15 inches
#220 and #400 sandpaper
gesso
acrylic or latex paint in color of your choice
antiquing glaze
instant decoupage (Fun Podge, Mod Podge, Decollage)
1 or 2 attractive magazine covers (old ones, if possible)
brayer
cigarette
decorative molding to go around the edges of the rack's feet (optional)
spray finish or varnish (optional)

Procedure

1. Cut out wood according to patterns. *See Diagram A.* Cut 4 side pieces and 2 facing pieces from ¼-inch wood, 1 bottom piece from ¼-inch wood, and 2 feet from ¾-inch wood. (See photograph for relative dimensions of pieces.)

2. Sand wooden pieces and washboard well, using coarser paper first and then finer.

3. Apply 2 coats of gesso to the washboard and to all of the wooden pieces, allowing adequate drying time between coats. Sand again in the same way.

4. Apply 2 coats of acrylic or latex paint to each piece, allowing adequate drying time between coats. (I painted my pieces before assembling them—an unusual procedure. I learned from sad experience that it's impossible to gesso and paint this project once it's assembled. If you do happen to nick the paint when you assemble this, simply touch up the nicked area.)

5. Assemble the rack. See *Diagram B.* Nail the feet to the outside of the vertical wooden washboard sides. Let the base of the feet extend 1½ inches below the bottom of the washboard. Nail the side pieces of the rack, on each side, front and back of the washboard, to the inner edges of the vertical wooden washboard sides. Nail the bottom piece in place under the metal washboard facings, directly to the bottom of the 4 side pieces. Nail the front and back facings through edges of side pieces, allowing equal overlap at top and bottom.

6. Apply antiquing glaze inside and outside the entire rack, following directions on the label. Wipe off excess with a paper towel.

7. Apply 2 coats of instant decoupage as a paint sealer over the entire rack, allowing adequate drying time between coats.

8. Trim a magazine cover to fit the rack front facing. Burn the edges of the cover with a cigarette to achieve an aged look *(optional)*. Apply 1 coat of instant decoupage as a glue to the back of the print and to the rack front facing. Carefully press the print onto the facing. Working on a small area at a time, roll out excess finish and air bubbles with a brayer over a slightly dampened paper towel. Roll from the center of the print to each of the 4 corners. If air bubbles develop, puncture them with a pin. Let dry. Repeat the same procedure on the rack back facing, if you wish.

9. To bury the print completely, thin the instant decoupage with water so it will flow on easily and apply 3 coats of finish over the print, allowing drying time between coats. Sand. Apply 3 more coats. Sand again.

10. *Optional:* Glue a decorative molding around the edges of the rack feet.

11. *Optional:* To give rack a fine-furniture look, apply 2 coats of varnish or spray finish over the entire rack, allowing adequate drying time between coats.

VARIATION 1: Substitute attractive sheet music covers (preferably old) and use rack for storing sheet music.

VARIATION 2: Paint the rack in a mod color. Substitute comic book covers, child's magazine covers, or sports or hobby magazine covers. Put in a child's room to store unusual-sized books.

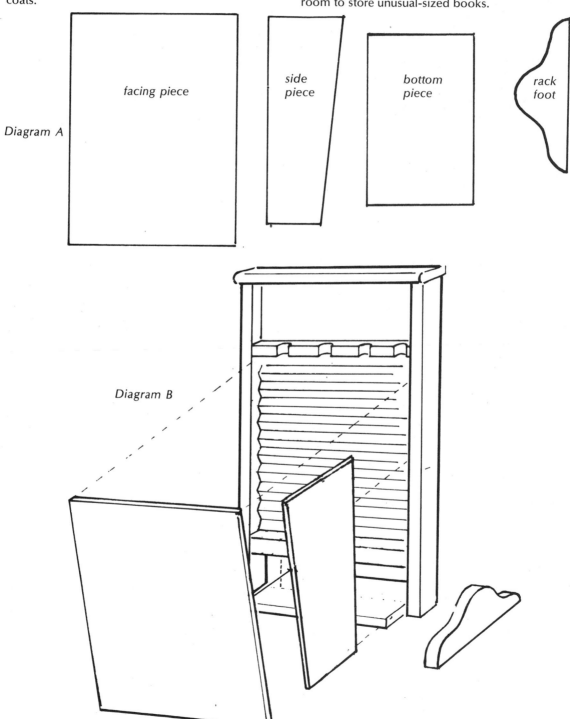

Diagram A

facing piece

side piece

bottom piece

rack foot

Diagram B

Gold Leaf Candy Jar

(See completed project on page 111.)

On a visit to a museum recently, I was attracted to an unusual diamond-trimmed gold leaf jar. Now I have a copy. True enough, my diamonds are rhinestones, and my gold braid is made from paper doilies. The glass candy jar I used is not even especially spectacular. You can purchase a duplicate of it in a dime store, hardware store, or department store. You may have one around the house.

The gold braid trim came from gold paper doilies left over from my mother and father's fiftieth wedding anniversary party. The rhinestones were trim I'd saved from an old evening dress. If you have a glass candy jar, some gold paper braid, and some old rhinestone trim, why not create this elegant-looking candy jar.

Materials

glass apothecary or candy jar, any size
ammonia
gold leaf adhesive* (a regular adhesive will dry too quickly)
packet of gold metal leaf*
sable hobby brush (label and use only for gold leaf work)
burnisher
gold leaf sealer*
light blue acrylic paint
white acrylic paint (optional)
soft sponge
decoupage sealer
gold paper doilies
gold decoupage braid
semi-gloss spray finish
white glue
rhinestones: old trim or by-the-yard

* These materials are available together in a gold-leafing kit, or they may be purchased separately.

Procedure

1. Wash candy jar and lid in ammonia and water solution. Clean and dry thoroughly.
2. Brush gold leaf adhesive lightly, but thoroughly, over the entire outside surface of the jar. (Do not apply gold leaf inside the jar. This is gold-leafing-on-glass in reverse: the gold will look as if it is inside the jar.) Leafing will not adhere to any surface not covered by adhesive. Wait 30 to 45 minutes, or until adhesive turns clear. Test the proper consistency by pressing your knuckle against surface; if you feel a slight clicking pull, adhesive is ready for gold leafing. (Note: Work in a room where there's not much traffic; a breeze will cause gold leaf particles to fly.)
3. Cut your gold leaf packet into 4 equal sections. Do not discard the protective paper that covers each piece of leaf in your packet; use it to lift and press the leaf in place on the jar. Apply the leaf to every area precoated with the adhesive; overlap pieces of gold leaf slightly. Lightly rub the leaf with the protective paper.
4. Allow the gold leaf to set for several hours. Use your clean, dry sable brush to smooth out the leaf with a patting or tapping motion of the brush and with smooth, even strokes. Remove the seams where a piece of leaf overlaps another by brushing lightly in a back and forth motion. Lightly rub along the surface with the burnisher to remove gold flakes.
5. Brush on 3 light coats of gold leaf sealer to protect the leaf from tarnishing. Let dry.
6. Prepare a very pale blue acrylic wash, mix blue acrylic paint with white if color is not light enough: dilute 1 part paint with 1 part water. Apply diluted paint over gold leaf in an antiquing effect with a dampened sponge; apply lightly so as not to hide gold. Let dry overnight.

7. Spray on 3 misty coats of decoupage sealer, allowing drying time between coats.

8. Seal paper doilies and decoupage braid with 3 misty coats of decoupage sealer. Separate sections of the doilies and work out your own design with the pieces on the jar.

9. Spray on 1 light coat of semi-gloss finish before applying braid. Glue decoupage braid on the top edge of the jar and the bottom edge of the jar lid. Glue sections of the paper doilies in place. Remove excess glue with a dampened cloth. After the glue has dried for a few hours, rub the braid with a burnisher, so the braid will not lift.

10. Spray on 2 or 3 misty coats of semi-gloss finish to protect the braid and paper trim.

11. Glue on rhinestones at indentations on the lid and at the base of the jar.

VARIATION: Make a silver anniversary gift, using silver leaf and silver braid. Dip gold braid in decoupage thinner to remove the gold finish and turn the braid silver.

Guest Towel Container

(See completed project on page 108.)

Don't throw away a leftover piece of hardware cloth or a small piece of heavy-duty screening. As small a piece as a 10-inch square will make a pretty container for your bathroom guest towels. A 16- inch square makes an unusual holiday centerpiece to fill with fresh greens or to display your holiday greeting cards. You can decorate your container in whatever color matches your decor, and you can make it in any size that suits needs.

Materials

10-inch square of hardware cloth or heavy-duty screening (<u>must</u> be a perfect square)
acrylic spray paint in color of your choice
2 yards velvet ribbon, ½ inch wide, in color of your choice
Velverette Craft Glue
covered wire
artificial or dried flowers to complement your color scheme
artificial bird

Procedure

1. Cut hardware cloth or screening to size.
2. Spray with a few misty coats of acrylic paint, allowing adequate drying time between coats. When thoroughly dry, turn to the opposite side and repeat the spraying procedure. (I use a deep cardboard carton for all spray painting.)
3. Cut 4 pieces of velvet ribbon, each 10 inches long. Apply glue to the back of the ribbon and to the edge of the screening, a section at a time. Crease the ribbon horizontally in the middle; press it along the edge of the screening, enfolding the edge inside. Continue until all edges of the screening are encased in velvet. Mitre corners where velvet overlaps.
4. Insert a piece of covered wire through 2 diagonal ends of the screening. Draw the 2 ends together toward the center. Tighten the wire and tie the ends of the wire together.
5. Make a bow of the remaining velvet ribbon; attach the bow to the center top with the covered wire. Insert dried or artificial flowers under the ribbon. Attach an artificial bird to the top with the same wire. Fold under exposed ends of wire to avoid accidents.

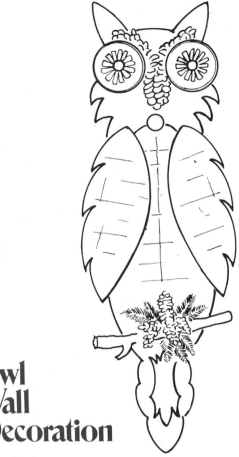

Owl Wall Decoration

(See completed project on page 54.)

I use an owl as the symbol of my shop, Craft Town. I have plaques, pocketbooks, jewelry, note paper, and even home furnishings that feature my favorite winged creature. If you're an owl lover, too, you'll enjoy a king-sized owl made from old wooden crates and salad bowls and pine cones. You can put this fellow beside the doorstep, near the entrance to the patio, or on a wall in your den or recreation room.

Materials

scrap lumber from sides of 3 orange crates, or wood left over from construction
2 old individual-size wooden salad bowls (for owl's eyes)
brush-on stain of your choice (I used walnut)
10 saw-head joint fasteners or a wooden strip, 4 inches × 18 inches
2 small wooden strips, ¾ inch × ¾ inch × ¼ inch
2 large artificial daisies
black acrylic paint
white glue

circular wooden cutting from tree branch, about ½-inch thick (for owl's mouth)
1 large pine cone, about 8 inches long
5 small pine cones, about 4 inches long
Y-shaped tree stick, about 15 inches long and 1½ inches diameter
several sprigs of artificial greens
saw-toothed metal picture hanger

Procedure

1. With a saw, cut out wood pieces according to patterns in *Diagram A* (if you are not expert at cutting wood, have your local lumberyard do this step). In addition, cut out 2 pieces of wood for back supports—one 4 inches × 9 inches × ⅜ inch, the other 4 inches × 12 inches × ⅜ inch. (Sand these pieces slightly, if you wish, though this isn't necessary because the owl should look rustic.)
2. Stain the above wood pieces and the salad bowls, following directions on the label. Wipe off excess with paper toweling.
3. Assemble the wooden pieces. See *Diagram B.* Use saw-head joint fasteners to connect the 2 body pieces on the back side. Join the 2 head pieces. Lay the head, body, and back tail in position. Center and nail the larger wooden support strip midway between the head and body. Center and nail the smaller support strip midway between the body and the tail. If you do not have joint fasteners (available in hardware stores), nail a thin wooden strip 4 inches wide along the entire length of the center back.
4. Turn the owl right side up and nail the wings in position. Note that the upper edges extend up about 1 inch into the head section.
5. Center and nail the front tail midway between the body section and the back tail.
6. Nail the two small strips of wood (¾ inch × ¾ inch × ¼ inch) to each side of the head at an outside point to be covered by the salad bowls when you nail them in place. This will tilt the bowls slightly inward. Nail the salad bowls in place.
7. Cut off the stems and leaves from the daisies. Paint their centers black. When dry, glue into the centers of the salad bowls.
8. Center and nail the owl's mouth (the circle cut from tree branch) midway between the head and the body.
9. Glue large pine cone between the salad bowl eyes, with the lower end directly above the mouth. Glue 2 of the smaller pine cones as brows over the eyes.

10. Nail Y-shaped tree stick horizontally, directly above the front tail. Center and glue 3 remaining small pine cones as feet resting on the stick. Crush them down a bit to resemble an owl's feet holding onto a branch. Nail them in place for additional support.

11. Tuck several sprigs of artificial greens under the stick.

12. Nail saw-toothed picture hanger center back on the top wooden support strip.

Diagram A

Diagram B

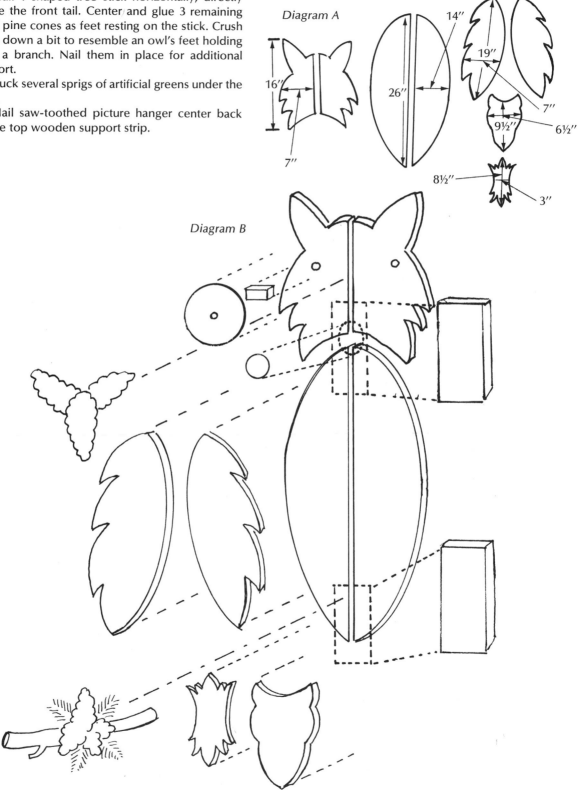

48

Meat Grinder Wall Plaque

(See completed project in photograph facing page 7.)

If you're lucky enough to have an old-fashioned meat grinder, don't throw it away. Filled with a few plastic vegetables, it makes a striking wall plaque for the kitchen. Even if you've given up your meat grinder in favor of a new model, you needn't pass up this project. Old-fashioned meat grinders are still available for little money at many hardware stores and thrift shops.

Materials

wood for plaque, 9 inches × 24 inches × ⅞ inch
wood for shelf, 4 inches × 6 inches × ⅞ inch
wood for bracket support: 2½ inches at widest
    part, 3½ inches long, 1 inch thick
#220 sandpaper
fruit wood stain
steel wool
acrylic paint in color of your choice
meat grinder
ammonia
spray finish or acrylic finish
small piece of Styrofoam to fit inside meat
    grinder
assorted plastic vegetables
heavy-duty stapler
decorative screw-type ring
saw-toothed metal picture hanger

Procedure

1. Cut curves at 4 corners of plaque piece. (A craft shop may have suitable wood pieces already cut, or you might take your plans to a lumberyard.) If you have a router, use it on the 4 edges of the plaque and on 3 edges of the shelf (the 2 shorter edges and 1 longer edge). Center and nail shelf 6 inches from bottom of plaque; nail bracket support to plaque, centering it under shelf; nail support to shelf.

2. Sand all wood well. Wipe with a soft cloth.

3. Apply stain to a dampened sponge. Wipe the wood, front and back (do not stain the decorative edges), with the stained sponge. Wipe off with paper toweling, then rub carefully with steel wool. Set aside to dry overnight.

4. Paint the decorative edges of the plaque with 2 coats of acrylic paint (I used green), allowing drying time between each coat. Let dry overnight.

5. Wash the meat grinder thoroughly with ammonia and soapy water to remove any grease. If you wish to keep a wooden handle natural, cover the handle with masking tape to prevent paint stains. You may touch up the handle with stain, if necessary.

6. Paint the meat grinder the same color as the decorative border. Apply 2 coats, allowing drying time between coats. Let dry overnight.

7. When thoroughly dry, spray the wood and the meat grinder with spray finish or acrylic spray. Allow to dry completely.

8. Attach the meat grinder tightly to the shelf with its own screw.

9. Insert a small piece of Styrofoam into the grinder opening. Insert the plastic vegetables into the Styrofoam. Attach larger vegetables directly to the plaque with a stapler.

10. Screw decorative ring to the center top edge of the plaque. Do not use this ring for hanging the plaque as it is not heavy enough to support the weight.

11. Attach picture hanger to back of plaque.

VARIATION: Follow the same procedure, but use an old-fashioned kitchen grater—with 4 sides—instead of the meat grinder. Substitute several wooden spoons and plastic fruits for the vegetables. Paint the spoons with 2 coats of acrylic paint. Insert Styrofoam at the base of the grater; insert ends of spoons into Styrofoam with spoon bowls coming through top of grater. Insert bunches of grapes into the openings in the grater sides. Center and nail a wooden block, slightly smaller than the wider open end of the grater, on the 4-inch × 6-inch wooden shelf. Place the wider end of the grater over this wooden support.

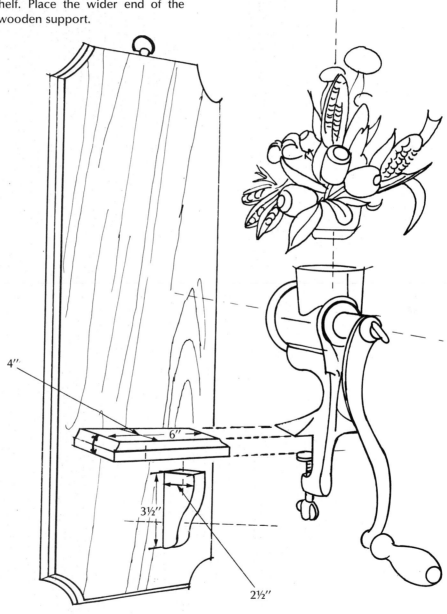

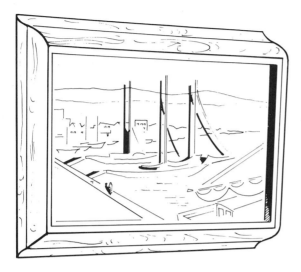

You may not have an old phonograph lid, but you can still make a fascinating picture. Find a pair of duplicate prints that appeal to you—perhaps from stationery, calendars, or greeting cards—and use a small drawer from an old desk or bureau for your frame. Start with something small to learn the techniques.

Materials

shadow box: old phonograph lid, small drawer from old desk, or if neither is available, wooden box with depth
ammonia
#220 sandpaper
wood putty (optional; if necessary to fill holes or repair damaged wood)
stain, or acrylic, or latex paint in color of your choice
steel wool (optional: if staining)
gesso (optional: if painting)
water-base paint remover (optional: for stripping old paint)
rubber gloves (optional: for use with paint remover)
antiquing glaze (optional)
clear varnish or instant spray finish
paste wax (optional)
pair of identical prints or illustrations to fit shadow box
backing cardboard cut to fit bottom of phonograph lid (not necessary if using drawer or wooden box)
decoupage sealer
decoupage or manicure scissors
waxed paper
Dow Corning Silicone Sealer
cardboard matting (optional)
glass to fit top of box
vinegar
old pair of clean cotton gloves
white glue
brown paper bag or brown wrapping paper (necessary for phonograph lid, same size as backing cardboard)
picture wire and 2 cup hooks
braid, ribbon, or braided string (optional: enough to fit around edges of glass)

Three-Dimensional Picture under Phonograph Lid
(See completed project on page 57.)

A man who had often accompanied his wife to our shop finally took up a craft of his own—three-dimensional decoupage. Since he had been a die-maker before his retirement, he was a natural for a craft that calls for careful cutting. I gave him a few basic instructions and two identical prints of a sailing ship. He came back with an absolutely delightful picture.

We then found an old phonograph lid to use as a shadow box for the picture. Before we framed the picture, he came up with the idea of using fine thread to indicate the ship's rigging. We matted the finished picture with cardboard and framed it under glass. We edged the glass on the phonograph lid frame with braided string. The result is a showpiece and a favorite of all visitors to our shop.

Procedure

1. Wipe the phonograph lid, the drawer, or the box with an ammonia and water solution to remove grease. (If you are using a drawer, remove the drawer pull, but don't throw it away; save it for another project.) Sand all sides well. Fill in holes with wood putty. Sand again.

If the wood is stained, you can renew finish with an application of matching stain, following directions on the label for application. Wipe off excess stain with a textured paper towel; allow to dry. Rub with steel wool.

If you wish to paint the wood, apply 1 coat of gesso (possibly 2, if the wood is poor, and sand between coats) over the old finish or unpainted wood. Allow to dry. Sand well. Apply 2 coats of acrylic paint, allowing drying time between coats.

If you wish to strip old paint, either to stain or repaint, use a water-base paint remover, following directions on the label. Work outdoors, if possible, and use rubber gloves.

If you want to antique the paint, apply antiquing glaze, according to directions on the label. Wipe off excess with a textured paper towel. Allow to dry overnight.

2. Apply 3 coats of clear varnish or instant spray finish, allowing drying time between coats. *Optional:* After the box is thoroughly dry (sometimes it takes up to several weeks, depending upon weather conditions), apply 1 coat of any good paste wax, waxing a small area at a time; rub well (a piece of a man's old felt hat is best for this purpose).

3. Study the prints carefully before you begin to work on them. One print will be a background print; the other, a cutting print. Determine which parts of the picture you wish to feature. Decide whether those parts would normally curve in an inward or outward direction.

4. Spray the back of your cutting print with 3 misty coats of decoupage sealer to make cutting easier. Glue the background print to the cardboard backing, or to inside of drawer or box.

5. Using decoupage or manicure scissors, cut out the pieces you plan to feature from your cutting print. Cut the inside areas before cutting outer edges. Cut with the curved point of the scissors pointed away from the print. Hold your cutting hand still, except to open and close scissor blades; with your other hand, feed the print into the scissor blades. Assemble pieces on waxed paper in the order that you will place them on the background print.

6. Contour or shape your cutouts as closely to their three-dimensional shape as possible. If they should curve inward (concave), hold them in the palm of your hand face up; if they should curve outward (convex), hold them face down. To shape them, use the back of a small spoon, the eraser end of a pencil, the smooth end of your burnisher, or the flat of your index fingernail. Gently press the piece down into the palm of your hand to give it the shape you desire.

7. In assembling cutout pieces, plan to work on 1 piece at a time. Be careful in handling cutouts after they are shaped. Squeeze out a little silicone sealer to the back of a cutout, pulling the tube away in the manner of the peak of a beaten egg white. Use tweezers to help in picking up and placing pieces. To apply sealer to tiny pieces, squeeze out a little onto waxed paper and apply with a toothpick.

8. Place the cutout over its duplicate area on the background print. Set down carefully to adhere it to the background print. Pull into position any area you might have flattened in gluing. Pick up excess adhesive with a toothpick immediately, and remove as quickly as possible with a damp paper towel any smudges of sealer on your background print. Continue placing the cutouts, one at a time, until your three-dimensional decoupage is completed.

9. *Optional:* If your shadow box is too large for your print, cut a cardboard matting with outward dimensions the same size as your shadow box. This will give you a border wide enough to compensate for the difference between the size of your print and the size of your box.

10. Wash the glass in a solution of vinegar and water; clean thoroughly and dry well. Handle with an old pair of clean cotton gloves to keep fingerprints off the surface. Using a brush, lightly apply white glue to the edges of the box. Allow the glue to set for a moment, then gently place the glass over the glued area and press down carefully. Let dry.

11. If you are using a phonograph lid, attach your print with masking tape to the bottom of the lid. Cut a brown paper bag or brown wrapping paper to fit the bottom of the lid. Glue the paper to all 4 sides of the cardboard backing. Insert cup hooks; attach picture wire for hanging.

12. *Optional:* Trim the edges of the glass with braid, ribbon, or braided string. If you are using gold braid, spray the braid with 3 misty coats of decoupage sealer to protect the color, allowing

52

drying time between each coat. Wipe the braid
with antiquing glaze and a damp sponge; remove
excess glaze with a textured paper towel. Allow to
dry completely. Cover the antiquing with 2 coats of
decoupage sealer, allowing drying time between
each coat. Cut the braid into 4 pieces, slightly
longer than the box sides.

Place the braid face down on waxed paper;
lightly apply white glue to the back of the braid and
allow to set until it becomes sticky. Center the braid
between the glass and the box sides; apply carefully, pressing down with fingertips and overlapping end pieces. Mitre corners by making a diagonal cut through the overlapped pieces. Cut and
attach ribbon in the same manner; mitre corners.

Belted Wastepaper Basket
(See completed project on page 57.)

In these diet-conscious days there may be someone you know who has a now-too-large but not-
too-worn belt. An oversized belt and a piece of
leftover fabric will make a beautiful wastepaper
basket, if you use them to cover an ordinary, inexpensive one. Depending on the fabric and the belt
you choose, you can make a wastepaper basket to
suit any decor. A wastepaper basket with a soldier
print will please a young son or nephew. A leather-
look plastic wastepaper basket will look great in a
den or office. A white brocade fabric or a moire
wallpaper and a gold belt will look elegant on a
wastepaper basket in a powder room.

Materials

metal wastepaper basket (if you have one in
   good condition, use it; if not, buy an
   inexpensive one)
instant decoupage (Fun Podge, Mod Podge,
   Decollage)
leftover drapery fabric, ½ to 1 yard (amount
   depends on basket size)
acrylic spray (optional)
edging of your choice to go around the top and
   bottom edges of the basket (burlap ribbon,
   Mystik Tape, decorative braid, fringe)
oversized belt, approximately 42 inches long
Dow Corning Urethane Bond Glue

Procedure

1. Make sure wastepaper basket is clean and in good repair. Wash, if necessary, and dry well.
2. Brush 1 coat of instant decoupage over the entire exterior of the basket. Let dry.
3. Examine fabric to select best arrangement of pattern. Cut fabric into 2 pieces—each piece the exact size of half of the basket, from side seam to side seam, and from top to bottom.
4. Starting at a side seam, apply a coat of instant decoupage to one quarter of the basket. Cover the glued area with fabric, rolling out bubbles with the palm of your hand. Do not stretch the fabric. Continue until the basket is covered with fabric. (The top and bottom edges of the fabric will be flush with the top and bottom of the basket; side seams will butt exactly.) Let fabric dry completely; the texture will feel quite hard to the touch when dry.
5. Apply 2 more coats of instant decoupage, allowing drying time between coats.
6. *Optional:* If you think the basket will get soiled and you will want to wash it, apply several coats of acrylic spray, allowing drying time between coats. (Instant decoupage will water-spot.)
7. Glue the edging of your choice around the top and bottom edges of the fabric.
8. Buckle a belt, and cut belt at point opposite the buckle. Glue the belt to cover the side seams of buckle. Glue 1 of belt pieces over each side seam of fabric so that the cut ends of belt will be flush with bottom of the wastepaper basket.

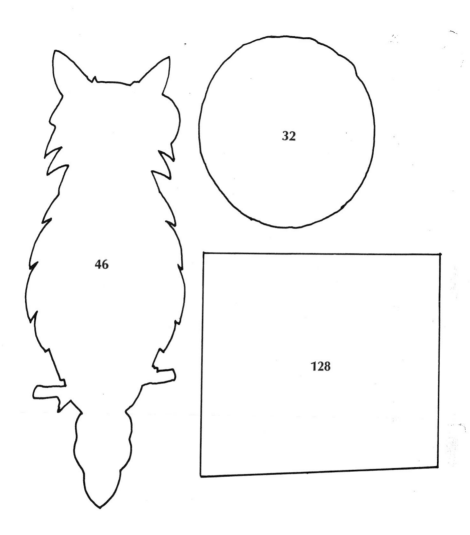

Details and instructions for projects shown may be found on page number indicated

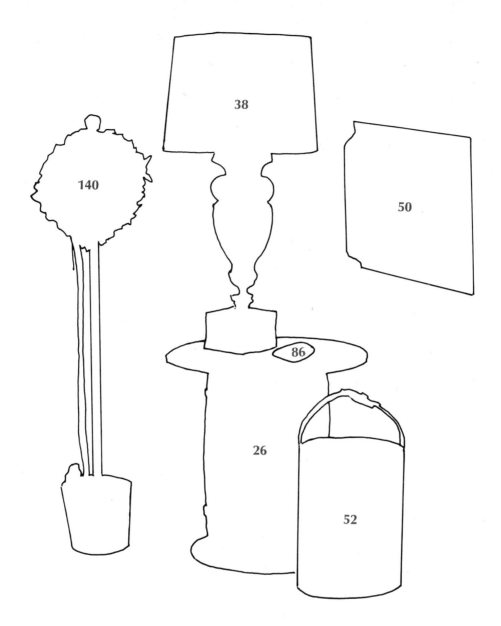

Details and instructions for projects shown may be found on page number indicated

Chapter
2

Gifts and Fundraisers

"How You Grow" Measuring Stick

(See completed project on page 7.)

If you still happen to have an old wooden bedslat, or even a long strip of scrap wood, you can make this "How You Grow" measuring stick for a child's room.

Materials

**wooden bedslat or strip of wood, 3¼ inches ×
    53 inches**
**gesso or decoupage sealer (depending upon
    roughness of slat)**
#220 sandpaper
**stain, or acrylic or latex paint in color of your
    choice**
**instant decoupage (Fun Podge, Mod Podge,
    Decollage)**
**gift wrapping paper, wallpaper, greeting cards,
    or fabric with interesting children's designs**
brayer
measuring tape
**rickrack, ribbon, or braid trim for edges
    (optional)**
clear acrylic spray

Procedure

1. Apply a coat of gesso, or 2 if needed, to the slat if it is rough. Sand when dry. If slat is in good condition, seal with a coat of decoupage sealer.
2. Brush on 2 coats of acrylic paint, allowing drying time between coats.
3. Paint slat with a coat of instant decoupage. Let dry.
4. If design permits, cut out strips of gift wrapping paper, wallpaper, or fabric to fit board, or cut out separate designs to be glued on the board. Apply another coat of instant decoupage to the board and attach the designs. Roll out excess glue and air bubbles with a brayer over a dampened paper towel. When thoroughly dry, brush on another coat of instant decoupage over the front of the board.
5. Use instant decoupage to glue a measuring tape vertically to a side of the board, or the middle, depending on your design. Be sure the lowest measure is at the bottom.
6. *Optional:* Glue rickrack or trim to the edges of the board.
7. Spray a coat of acrylic spray over the entire board.

VARIATION: Substitute felt cutouts for paper.

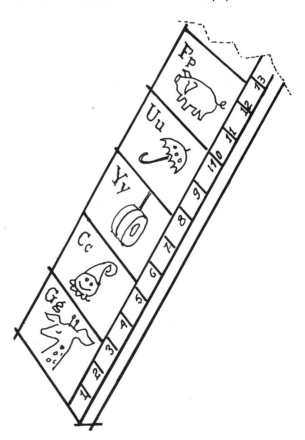

½ yard leftover fabric
instant decoupage (Fun Podge, Mod Podge, Decollage)
brayer
Velverette Craft Glue
3 yards guimpe braid, in color of your choice (I used white)
movable eye
piece of #10 mono canvas, 6 inches × 8 inches
several strands of needlepoint yarn, in color of your choice (I used pink)
stitchery needle
white felt, 6 inches × 8 inches
½ yard felt, in color of your choice (I used pink)
saw-toothed metal picture hanger
decoupage spray finish (optional)

Child's Clothes Hanger

(See completed project on page 7.)

"I never forget to hang up my clothes," boasts this clothes hanger, which is a great gift for a favorite child. Older children enjoy making this project for younger siblings; they need adult help on construction, but they do a masterful job of decorating it.

My elephant is prim, proper, and ladylike, covered with pink gingham and trimmed in shiny white guimpe braid; in fact, it matches the doll cradle in this chapter. But the elephant can be decorated any way you choose.

Materials

scrap wood, 14 inches × 18 inches × ⅜ inch (for elephant) and 5½ inches × 7¼ inches × ¼ inch (for ear)
3 ½-inch dowels, 3½ inches high
1 ½-inch dowel, 3¾ inches high
drill (if you don't own one, you can borrow a friend's)
#220 sandpaper
gesso
white acrylic paint

Procedure

1. Cut elephant body and ear according to the diagram, or have someone cut them for you.
2. Drill a hole for the ½-inch dowel in the elephant's ear 2¼ inches up from the bottom of the ear and centered; drill completely through wood. Drill 4 holes for the dowels in the elephant's body in a line 7½ inches down from the straight edge top of the body. Start the first hole 2 inches in from the left side; make each of the 3 succeeding holes 3 inches to the right of the last hole drilled. Be sure the holes are tight enough for the dowels to fit snugly.
3. Sand all edges well.
4. Apply a coat of gesso over all areas of the wood and dowel sticks. Let dry and sand lightly.
5. Paint ear and dowels with 2 coats of white acrylic paint, allowing drying time between coats.
6. Make a pattern for fabric by covering the elephant's body with a piece of aluminum foil, extending the foil ½ inch over to the back. Press the foil against the edges of the wood and the dowel hole openings. Cut out foil pattern. Cut out fabric according to foil pattern; cut away hole openings, where foil indentations appear.
7. Brush a coat of instant decoupage over the dowel sticks, the elephant's ear, and on the front of the body, the sides, and the ½-inch turnover area (for fabric) on the back edge. Let dry.
8. Brush another coat of instant decoupage over the same areas on the elephant's body. Brush one coat on the back of the fabric and attach the fabric

to the wood, keeping dowel hole openings even; press the fabric around the sides to the back. Remove excess glue and air bubbles with a brayer over a dampened paper towel, rolling from the center out to each of the 4 corners. Let dry overnight.

9. Glue ear in place on the body, lining up the 2 dowel holes. Put glue on the ends of the dowels and insert dowels into drilled holes, gluing the 3¾-inch dowel into the ear. Let glue dry.

10. Glue guimpe braid around the dowel holes, around the edges of the ear, and around the side edges of the body.

11. Glue a movable eye on the elephant's ear.

12. On needlepoint canvas, pencil in lettering for stitchery on what will be the elephant's blanket. Print "I never forget to hang up my clothes," and stitch with a cross stitch or split and back stitch.

13. Put glue on the edges of the back of the canvas and glue canvas to the white felt. When it is secure, glue the back of the felt to the elephant's body, directly above the first 3 dowel holes. Glue guimpe braid around the 4 edges of the canvas.

14. Cover the back of the elephant with felt, using aluminum foil to shape the pattern. Glue felt.

15. Nail picture hanger to the center back of the elephant near the top.

16. *Optional:* For protection, spray front of elephant with a misty coat of decoupage spray finish.

VARIATION: Instead of covering the elephant with fabric, and trimming with braid and needlepoint canvas, you may decorate your elephant entirely with paint. I have seen a marvelous elephant painted imaginatively in red, white, and blue for a little boy's room.

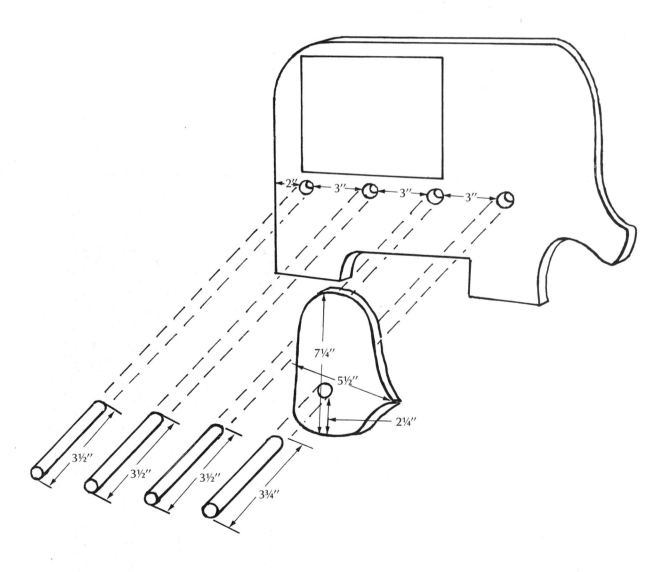

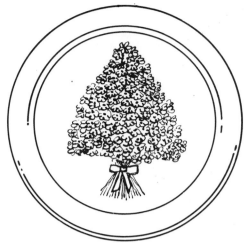

Drapery Ring Picture Frame

Don't throw away an old or extra wooden drapery ring. It can become a lovely frame for a miniature picture made from dried flowers, bits of fabric, shirt cardboard, and a brown paper bag. You can hang several of these tiny pictures on a ribbon as an arrangement. Individually or in a grouping, they are ideal as gifts or fundraisers.

For drying your garden flowers, use Flower-dri or Silica gel and follow directions on the label. Roses, marigolds, pansies, and violets, all dry beautifully in Flower-dri in just a few days. Don't throw away the statice or baby's breath you might receive in a commercial flower arrangement. Remove them from water and let them air-dry. If you haven't a garden, use skyrockets and bunches of various dried flowers that you can obtain very inexpensively at craft shops, florists, dime stores, and supermarkets.

Materials

wooden drapery ring
vinegar (optional)
acrylic paint or stain in color of your choice (optional)
spray finish or acrylic spray
cardboard to fit inside ring
fabric to cover cardboard: velvet, moire, brocade, taffeta, burlap, or felt
dried flowers of your choice
white glue
small piece of velvet or burlap ribbon, ⅛ to ¼ inch wide
decoupage sealer
brown paper bag
paste-on picture holder (optional: for an individual picture)
velvet ribbon long enough and wide enough to allow borders on all sides of frames (optional: for arrangement of several pictures)
decorative ring or wooden dowel hanger (optional)

Procedure

1. If drapery ring has been used, wipe with a vinegar and water solution to remove grease.
2. Apply 2 coats of acrylic paint to the ring, allowing drying time between coats, or wipe on the stain of your choice, wiping off excess stain with a paper towel. Allow to dry completely.
3. Spray newly painted or stained ring with spray finish or acrylic spray. Let dry.
4. Place the wooden ring on cardboard. Make a pencil line around the outside edges. Cut cardboard according to pattern. Set ring aside.
5. Cut fabric to the exact size of the cardboard. Glue fabric to the cardboard.
6. Plan your dried flower arrangement on a piece of paper the same size as the cardboard circle. Work with the arrangement until it pleases you; then move it over piece by piece with tweezers onto the fabric-covered cardboard.
7. Apply a bit of glue to the back of each flower and glue in place. Glue dried stems to the bottom of the arrangement, slanting them toward the center.
8. With a small piece of narrow ribbon, make a tiny bow. Cut a piece of ribbon horizontally if it is too wide. Glue ribbon bow in place over the stems.
9. Spray a misty coat of decoupage sealer over the arrangement.
10. Glue the edges of the drapery ring as a frame around the arrangement.
11. Cut a backing piece from the paper bag to fit up to the outside edges of the ring. Glue to the back of the ring. Let dry.

12. *Optional:* Attach a paste-on picture holder to the back of the frame if using as a single picture.

13. *Optional:* Gather the top edge of a strip of velvet ribbon (length will be determined by the number of frames you intend to use on it) around a decorative ring hanger. Or glue the top edge of a strip of ribbon to a dowel hanger slightly wider than the width of the ribbon strip. Plan placement of frames; glue frames in place.

Decoupaged Aluminum Skillet

If you have an old aluminum skillet that is worn too thin to use for cooking, don't throw it away. Instead, refinish it, decoupage a picture and a favorite recipe on it, and hang it on the kitchen wall. This makes a fine kitchen shower gift, too, when you share a special recipe with the bride.

Materials

aluminum skillet
vinegar
copper finish (Rub 'n Buff, Lustre Wax, Liquid Copper)
turpentine
Treasure Sealer or decoupage sealer
instant decoupage (Fun Podge, Mod Podge, Decollage)
recipe
black India ink (optional)
white acrylic paint (optional)
magazine, seed catalog, old cookbook, or greeting card picture of favorite food
brayer
acrylic spray
leather thong for hanging skillet

Procedure

1. Wash skillet with a solution of vinegar and water to remove grease.

2. Squeeze a small amount of copper finish into a piece of aluminum foil, thin with turpentine, and brush on skillet. Do not apply heavily; one application is usually enough. (Apply several thin coats if you are not satisfied with coverage, allowing a few seconds drying time between coats and sealing with Treasure Sealer or decoupage sealer between coats.) Let dry. Buff with a soft cloth to a lustrous finish.

3. Apply coat of sealer. Let dry.

4. Brush coat of instant decoupage over the pan. Let dry.

5. Copy a favorite recipe on paper; print or write in India ink, or use your typewriter. Seal India ink or typing with a coat of decoupage sealer. If you cut out a magazine recipe, cover the printing on the back with white acrylic paint.

6. Cut out a picture to complement the recipe of your choice. If printing appears on the back, paint back with white acrylic paint.

7. Brush another coat of instant decoupage on the skillet. Apply a coat of instant decoupage to the back of the picture and the recipe; glue to the skillet. Roll out excess glue and air bubbles with a brayer over a dampened paper towel. If an air bubble develops, prick with a pin and roll again. Let dry.

8. Spray skillet with a coat of acrylic spray.

9. Attach a leather thong through the handle for hanging. Knot the ends of the thong.

Papier-Mâché Turtle

(See completed project on page 173.)

Papier-mâché animals, fruits, and figures are easy to do and fun to make, a joy to receive, and popular items at a bazaar booth. Old newspapers, the basis of papier-mâché figures are certainly easy enough to come by. Once you learn the techniques of making a papier-mâché figure, you can duplicate practically any shape you wish and paint it whatever color appeals to you. A personable papier-mâché turtle (I named mine Sam) is a good figure with which to start.

Materials

newspaper
masking tape
aluminum foil
Celluclay (instant papier-mâché)
white glue
gesso
acrylic paints: moss green, red, blue, and gold
    (or colors of your choice)
Dow Corning Silicone Sealer
antiquing glaze of your choice
crystal clear glaze or acrylic spray
felt to cover bottom of turtle (I used green)

Procedure

1. Roll up several sheets of newspaper. Pull and bunch one end toward to elongate and shape turtle head and nose; see diagram. Wrap masking tape to tighten and secure neck area. Bunch the remaining end of the newspaper roll into a ball with a flat bottom. Add crumpled newspaper to make the body of the turtle bigger, keeping the bottom area flat. Work with the paper until you are satisfied that it looks like a turtle shape.

2. Wrap masking tape all around the bunched newspaper. Be sure the bottom is still flat when you are finished.

3. Wrap aluminum foil over the entire turtle to hold the shape.

4. Mix half a package of Celluclay according to package directions, adding 2 tablespoons glue to give it more body. To make it easier to work with, let set overnight in the refrigerator.

5. Spread Celluclay mixture over the entire aluminum-covered shape. Mound it over the top; keep the texture irregular. When satisfied with the shape, put it aside to dry thoroughly. This may take several days, depending on the weather.

6. When thoroughly dry, brush on a coat of gesso over the turtle. Let dry.

7. Apply 2 coats of green acrylic paint to the turtle, allowing drying time between coats.

8. Screw the top with the smaller opening on the tube of silicone sealer (there is a choice of 2 tops in each package). Squeeze out sealer over the body of the turtle in a free design, or make a design of your choice, outlining the edges of the design with a thin line of sealer.

9. Paint the silicone sealer outlines in gold and the swirl designs in between in alternating red and blue tones. Let dry thoroughly (48 hours or longer). (See photograph on page 173.)

10. Apply antiquing glaze over the turtle. Wipe off excess with a textured paper towel. Allow 24 hours drying time.

11. Spray on a coat of crystal clear glaze or acrylic spray. Let dry.

12. Cut felt to size and shape of the bottom of the turtle. Glue to the base.

VARIATION: Use an already-formed shape to shape your papier-mâché figure. I bought an over-ripe watermelon and used it to form a papier-mâché watermelon. When the instant papier-mâché had dried around the watermelon, I cut it in half with a knife, removed the watermelon, and taped it together again.

Step 1

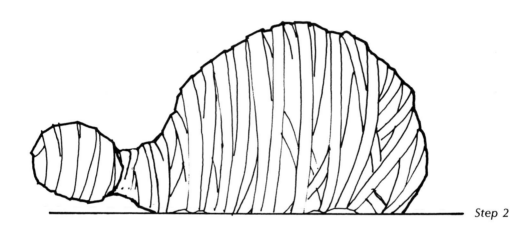

Step 2

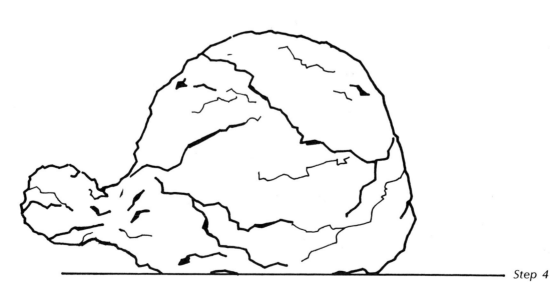

Step 4

66

Coffee Can Cookie Jar (See completed project on page 111.)

Don't throw away an empty 3-pound coffee can. You can make a most inviting cookie jar from it. Paint the can and decorate the sides with a favorite cookie shape (I used gingerbread men). Make a lid out of wood (this is what I did), or cut a lid from a piece of cork, or reinforce the plastic top that comes with the coffee can. Then, all you'll need to do is fill the can with your favorite cookies, and your home will be a house with a cookie jar.

Materials

3-pound coffee can
vinegar
#220 sandpaper
gesso (optional)
acrylic paint in <u>base</u> color of your choice (I used yellow) or Rustoleum
acrylic paints in <u>trim</u> colors of your choice (I used orange, brown, and white)
gingerbread boy cookie cutter, or any other cookie cutter figures you desire
1 sheet Formare, 9- × 11-inch size (this is a new craft material that can be cut and shaped to any contour)
acrylic spray
wooden circle cut to fit can diameter (you can cut your own lid or purchase one in a craft store, lumberyard, and some hardware and department stores; some lids come with handles attached)
small circular drawer pull, wood or china, for lid handle

Procedure

1. Wash can in a solution of vinegar, soap, and water to remove grease and coffee grounds. Dry.
2. Sand outside of can well.
3. *Optional:* If you're going to use acrylic paint, apply coat of gesso to the outside of the can. (This is not necessary if you plan to use Rustoleum.) Let dry. Sand lightly.
4. Apply 2 coats of yellow acrylic paint (or color of your choice) to the outside of the can. Or you may apply several coats of Rustoleum. Let dry, allowing adequate drying time between coats. Sand lightly.
5. Paint the metal edges at the top and bottom of the can with orange paint (or color of your choice). Let dry.
6. Place gingerbread cookie cutter (or cutter in figure of your choice) on sheet of Formare and trace outline with pencil; repeat 4 times. Cut out gingerbread men with scissors. Shape the cutouts to the curve of the can; remove from can.
7. Paint gingerbread men brown; trim edges and features with white paint.
8. Spray gingerbread men with several misty coats of acrylic spray.
9. Glue gingerbread men in 4 places around the outside of the can, spacing an equal distance apart.
10. Cut a wooden circle to fit can top or have one cut for you. Sand well, rounding top edge of circle; keep bottom edge flat.
11. Brush a coat of gesso on both sides of the lid. Let dry. Sand lightly.
12. Apply 2 coats of orange acrylic paint (or color of your choice) to both sides of the lid, allowing adequate drying time between coats. Paint handle in your base color if it is wood; do not paint if you are using a china drawer pull.
13. With a pencil, print or write "A Home Is a House with a Cookie Jar" on the lid. Go over printing or writing with orange acrylic paint. (Don't be concerned if your letters are not perfect; rustic letters will add charm.) Let dry completely.

14. Spray can, lid handle (if wood), and lid with several misty coats of acrylic spray.

15. Attach handle to center of lid with a nail or screw.

VARIATION: Use Christmas cookie cutters to cut Formare and decorate figures and can in holiday colors. Fill can with home-baked cookies and give as a Christmas gift.

Bird Seed Container (See completed project on page 111.)

Don't throw away metal boxes and cans with lids in which candy, cookies, pretzels, potato chips, and tobacco are sometimes packaged. Make a repoussé-decorated container to hold bird seed— or anything else you want it to hold.

Materials

metal can with lid
vinegar
tole primer or Rustoleum
#220 sandpaper
acrylic paint in color of your choice
antiquing glaze of your choice
2 bird prints (each of my prints had 2 birds)
decoupage sealer
decoupage or manicure scissors
soft cloth pad
white glue
bread dough: 3 slices white bread, 3 tablespoons white glue, 3 drops glycerine, 3 drops lemon juice
spray varnish

Procedure

1. Wash can with vinegar and water to remove grease. Dry. Remove handle from lid.

2. Spray can and lid with 1 coat of tole primer or Rustoleum, following directions on the can. Allow to dry thoroughly. Sand.

3. Paint with 2 coats of dark-colored acrylic paint or 3 coats of a pastel shade. Allow adequate drying time between coats.

4. Apply antiquing glaze; wipe off excess with textured paper towel. Attach handle.

5. To protect colors in bird prints from running or fading, seal prints with 3 misty coats of decoupage sealer, allowing drying time between coats.

6. Hold one print against a window. On the back, pencil the outline and details of the birds' bodies. Repeat for other print.

7. Carefully cut out prints with decoupage or manicure scissors. Check places that you intend to stretch to give depth to the birds' bodies.

8. Soak each print in water until soft, about 30 seconds. Place print face down on a soft pad. (Save old ironing board pads.) Using your pencil lines as a guide, push down on print with your pencil eraser tip. When you have stretched the cavity of each bird's body enough, allow to dry thoroughly. Repeat for other print.

9. Dilute white glue with water and apply several coats to each print, allowing drying time between coats.

10. Prepare bread dough mixture. Remove crusts, tear bread into small pieces, and place in a bowl. Add glue, glycerine, and lemon juice. Mix together with fingers. Knead until mixture has a smooth texture and does not stick to fingers. Store in plastic bag and refrigerate overnight.

11. Fill the cavity of the bird with the bread dough mixture to within ⅛ inch.

12. Glue the birds to the front and back sides of the can. Allow to dry.

13. Spray with 3 misty coats of varnish, allowing adequate drying time between coats.

Daisy Mirror

(See completed project on photograph facing page 1.)

Don't throw away leftover pieces of insulation board. Even if you're not artistically inclined, you can make a pretty daisy mirror. An art teacher in our shop uses this easy project to convince her beginner students that simple decorative painting is not limited to artists but is really a craft technique that everyone can learn.

Materials

insulation board, 20 inches × 14 inches × ½ inch
#220 sandpaper
X-acto knife
gesso
tracing paper
graphite paper
acrylic paints: white, gold, moss green, red, and black
spray finish or acrylic spray
mirror glass, 7 inches × 8 inches × ⅛ inch
felt or wallpaper, 20 inches × 14 inches
saw-toothed metal picture hanger

Procedure

1. Copy design for daisy mirror (see dotted lines on diagram) onto insulation board; cut out with saw (or have this done for you). Cut out circle for mirror glass, 6½ inches in diameter where indicated on diagram, and cut out 3 triangular sections near leaves. Lightly sand rough edges.

2. On the back of the board, using the mirror opening to determine centering, draw a rectangle 7 inches wide and 8 inches long for the mirror glass. With an X-acto knife, cut a groove ⅛ inch deep to insert mirror and to permit it to lie flush with back of board. Cut away the top ⅛-inch layer within this rectangle.

3. Apply 2 coats of gesso over the front of the board and over all edges, allowing drying time between coats. Sand lightly.

4. With a pencil, draw the details of the daisy: petals, leaves, ladybug. (Refer to photograph. Draw the petals and leaf outlines freehand. Trace the ladybug by placing tracing paper over the diagram. Copy your traced or freehand picture over graphite paper onto the insulation board.)

5. If you use acrylic paint from a jar, dip your brush into the jar and paint directly on the board. If you use acrylic paint from a tube, squeeze some out onto a plastic lid (don't throw away plastic container lids!); thin paint with water to the consistency of heavy cream and then paint. Paint the areas you have penciled in the following colors:

> daisy petals: white
> leaves and stem: green
> ladybug: red with white dots, black head and black feelers
> ¼-inch border around the edges of the open circle: gold
> small area near the gold border between each petal: light green (lighten green with white)

Be sure to extend your colors over the edges of the mirror. Do not try to be too professional in your painting; in decorative painting you are striving for a rough, rustic look.

6. Dry-brush each petal with gold and dry-brush the leaves and stem with white for shading. To dry brush, dip your brush into the paint and remove as much excess paint as possible; brush back and forth several times on paper until the paint has a faint, streaky look. Brush lightly to shade. Let paint dry.

7. Check photograph facing page 1 for detail lines. In black, paint petal outlines, leaf outlines, outline of ladybug, and short lines over gold center border. Let paint harden for 3 days.

8. Spray the mirror with 3 misty coats of spray finish or acrylic spray, allowing drying time between coats. Be sure to spray edges well so that they do not chip with use.

9. Placing masking tape all around, attach mirror from the back in the grooved area prepared for it.

10. Cut felt or wallpaper in the outline of the daisy, using your original pattern. Cut out the 3 triangular sections, but do not cut out the center opening. Glue felt or wallpaper to back of the board.

11. Attach a saw-toothed metal hanger to the back of the board.

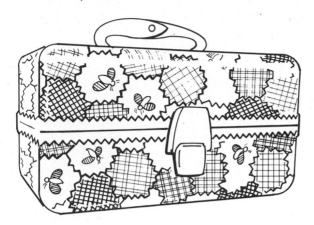

Tackle Box Sewing Basket

(See completed project on page 4.)

Don't throw away an old metal tackle box or pass one by at a garage sale. Covered with fabric print, it can make a marvelously roomy sewing box.

Materials

metal tackle box
vinegar
wire brush or steel wool or Rustoleum (optional: for rust removal)
gesso
#220 sandpaper (optional: if necessary)
acrylic spray paint for inside of box in color compatible with fabric used outside
instant decoupage (Fun Podge, Mod Podge, Decollage)
leftover fabric scraps to cover outside of box in quilt pattern
waxed paper or plastic sheeting
brayer
trim for box edges in 2 colors of your choice: rickrack, braid, or ribbon
Velverette Craft Glue
acrylic spray (optional)

Procedure

1. Wash tackle box with solution of vinegar and water.

2. Remove rust, if any, with a wire brush or piece of steel wool. If rust persists, apply Rustoleum, following directions on the can.

3. Apply 1 coat of gesso over the entire box, inside and outside. If the box is in poor condition, apply a second coat and sand between coats.

4. Spray inside of box with 2 misty coats of acrylic paint, allowing adequate drying time between coats.

5. Apply coat of instant decoupage over the inside of the box. When dry, apply coat to the outside of the box.

6. Brush instant decoupage over the scraps of fabric, keeping waxed paper or plastic sheeting underneath. Lift the fabric before it dries so that it does not stick to the waxed paper. When dry, turn the fabric and repeat the procedure on the other side. Let dry. Your fabric scraps will now cut easily without raveling.

7. Cut fabric scraps into enough patchwork squares to cover outside of box.

8. Apply a coat of instant decoupage to a small section of the box, and to the back of the fabric that will cover that section. Glue the fabric to the box, overlapping fabric, if you wish; roll out excess glue and air bubbles with a brayer. Continue the procedure until the entire outside of the box is covered with fabric in a patchwork pattern. Wash brayer with soap and water when finished.

9. Glue trim around the edges of each patchwork square and contrasting trim to long edges of box with Velverette Craft Glue. Apply a coat of instant decoupage over the trim.

10. *Optional:* If there is a possibility of soiling, apply a coat of acrylic spray over entire box. (Remember that instant decoupage shows water spots.)

VARIATION 1: Instead of covering outside of box with fabric squares, you may prefer a solid piece of fabric. Make a tracing paper pattern of the outside of your box. If you have enough fabric in one piece, plan to cut one large piece to go all around the box and 2 separate pieces for the top and bottom. Place your tracing paper pattern on the fabric, positioning it to make the best use of your fabric design. Cut fabric, and proceed with step 8 above. Glue trim around the edges of the box and apply instant decoupage over the trim.

VARIATION 2: A metal tackle box makes a marvelous jewelry box. Follow all the directions for applying fabric, perhaps to match your bedroom draperies or bedspread. Or you can paint the outside of the box instead of covering it with fabric. Line the inside of the box with velveteen or felt, making the lining pattern from aluminum foil.

VARIATION 3: Use spray paint inside and outside the tackle box to make a handyman's tool kit or a box for artist's supplies. Apply appropriate cutouts with instant decoupage.

Tin Can Miniatures

(See completed project on page 134.)

Don't throw away an empty tuna fish can. Wash it well, decorate it with bits of leftover ribbon and lace, and add your favorite miniatures to make a hostess gift or table decoration.

Materials

empty tuna fish can
vinegar
gesso
acrylic paint in color of your choice
white glue
net or lace to encircle the outside of the can
½-inch velvet ribbon to encircle the can 4 times
ruffled piece of net or lace to encircle outside of can
¼-inch velvet ribbon in contrasting or accent color to encircle can once
Stickum
small piece of moss for base of can
small piece of statice or any dried weed or twig
wooden or ceramic miniature
dried flower, such as skyrocket or starflower
pearl trim, ¾ yard (optional)

Procedure

1. Remove bottom of can with can opener. Remove label. Wash can well with vinegar and water and dry thoroughly.
2. Bend the can into a triangular shape, rounding the sides and flattening the bottom.
3. Apply gesso inside and outside the can. Allow to dry thoroughly.
4. Paint the can inside and outside with acrylic paint; allow to dry completely.
5. Glue the flat piece of lace around the outside of can, beginning at the base so that seams are not obvious.
6. Glue the ½-inch velvet ribbon flush with the 2 inside edges and 2 outside edges of can.
7. Glue the ruffled piece of lace or net around the outside of the can, and tie bow on top.
8. Center and glue the ¼-inch velvet ribbon over the ruffled trim. (Be careful not to get excess glue on trim. I find it helpful to squirt a bit of glue on a piece of plastic or aluminum foil and apply glue with a toothpick to the ribbon.) Tie bow on top.
9. Attach a piece of Stickum to the inside base of the can. Cover with moss. Roll another piece of Stickum into a tiny ball (enough to hold the statice or twig upright), and cover it with a bit of moss. Insert the statice into the moss-covered Stickum and place it on the mossy base.
10. Arrange your miniature and dried flower to suit yourself.
11. *Optional:* When everything is dry, glue pearl trim around the edge of the can. Make a tiny pearl bow and glue it to the top of the can.

VARIATIONS: Make this project for any holiday decoration. Easter miniatures could be chicks, ducks, and rabbits. Christmas miniatures could be Santa Claus, angels, elves.

Apple Basket Handbag

(See completed project on page 80.)

Take a good look at an apple basket. If you turn it upside down, it could be a lampshade. Turn it right side up and put a lid on it, and it can make a great handbag. If you then line it with a piece of fabric to match a dress you've made and you paint the top with cutouts that match the lining, you'll have a real designer's purse.

Materials

wooden apple basket
wood for lid, lid support strip, and handle
support strips
Dow Corning Urethane Bond Glue
hinges for basket lid
decoupage sealer
acrylic paint in white, green, black, and colors of
your print lining
Antiquing Foam or an antiquing product of your
choice with a black tone
tracing paper
graphite paper
Formare (if not available, use heavy cardboard)

spray finish or acrylic spray
leftover fabric for lining
guimpe braid in color of your choice to go
around the basket 3 times
2 screw rings
chain handle: whatever size suits your needs

Procedure

1. Cut out wooden pieces for the 2 sections of the basket lid. Then cut out a section slightly smaller than the unhinged half-moon area of the lid—this will be used to support that area of the lid. Last, cut out 2 small half-moon shapes just large enough to accommodate the screw rings. These, which will later be covered with guimpe braid, will be used to support the handles. Sand all edges well.

2. Glue lid support strip to inside half-moon area of basket lid. Use small nails for extra support.

3. Glue handle supports to outside basket sides, spacing them so that they are equidistant from the center of the lid support strip. Place small nail in each.

4. Glue half-moon section of lid over support strip.

5. Sand entire basket; rub well with steel wool.

6. Seal basket inside and out with decoupage sealer.

7. Brush 2 coats white acrylic paint on basket outside, inside basket lid, all inside edges, and inside wooden support strip. Allow drying time after each coat.

8. Apply antiquing foam heavily with a dampened sponge. Let set for a few minutes, wipe off excess with a textured paper towel, and let dry. (Basket should now have a gray pewter look.)

9. Copy pattern of leaves on tracing paper. (See page 180.) Trace over graphite paper onto top of lid. (Do not use carbon; it will smear.) Paint leaves with green acrylic paint; outline edges and veins in black.

10. Trace pattern of flower with tracing paper. Then trace pattern 3 times over graphite paper onto the textured side of Formare or heavy cardboard. Cut out the 3 flowers.

11. Paint flower petals in colors of your choice. Extend paint color of petal over edges of cutout. Outline each petal with black acrylic paint. Let paint harden for 3 days before applying finish.

12. Spray basket and cutout separately with 3 misty coats of acrylic spray or spray finish, allowing drying time between coats.

13. Apply glue to back of cutout with fingers or a brush. When it has become tacky to the touch, re-spread glue over the entire surface and press cutout down on lid of basket. Wipe off excess with a damp cloth. Cover with waxed paper, place a weight on it, and allow to set for 12 to 24 hours.

14. Press aluminum foil along sides of basket below wooden support strip inside basket to make pattern for basket side lining. Plan to make side lining in one piece. Cut foil. Cut fabric according to foil pattern, adding ½ inch on all edges.

15. Press aluminum foil around bottom of basket to make bottom lining pattern. Cut foil. Cut a cardboard circle the same size as the foil pattern. Cut fabric lining same size as cardboard, adding an extra ½ inch around the edges of the circle. Glue the ½-inch fabric turn-under to the reverse side of the cardboard.

16. Overlap the side seams of the side lining ½ inch, and glue down overlap, turning under raw edge of seam. Press under ½ inch on top edges of lining, and glue the ½-inch turn-under to sides of basket underneath the inside wooden support strip.

17. Glue the fabric-covered bottom lining circle to the bottom of the basket, covering the bottom edges of the basket side lining as you glue.

18. Glue guimpe braid around the outside wooden strips of the basket and along the inside support strip.

19. Hinge basket lid: Set the larger section of the lid in place on the basket; hold the 2 sections of lid together with masking tape. Place hinges on the top of the lid equally distant from both edges. Mark screw holes with a pencil. Remove the hinges; start holes for screws with an awl. Place the hinges again; set in screws about halfway; then go back and tighten screws. Remove masking tape.

20. Attach a chain handle to 2 screw rings, and attach the rings to the handle support strips on the side of the basket.

"Diamond" Paper Clip

Paper clips made from pinch-type clothespins and rhinestones are a fundraiser's best money-maker. If you haven't thrown away your old rhinestone jewelry, you can make several of these paper clips, attach them to small clipboards and pads of paper, and have a sure sellout. Ask your committee members to bring in their old jewelry. Old beads or pearls can be used as well as rhinestones.

Materials

pinch clothespin
silver Liquid Leaf, Rub 'n Buff, or Lustre Wax (with last two products, you'll need turpentine and aluminum foil)
Treasure Sealer
old jewelry: rhinestones, pearls, beads
Velverette Craft Glue
small clipboard (optional)
small pad of note paper (optional)

Procedure

1. Paint clothespin with two coats of Liquid Leaf, allowing drying time between coats. Or mix Lustre Wax or Rub 'n Buff with turpentine on a piece of aluminum foil; thin to the consistency of sour cream, and brush on; buff gently with a soft cloth.

2. Brush or spray on 2 coats of Treasure Sealer, allowing drying time between coats.

3. On the outside edges of the clothespin, glue on jewelry with Velverette Craft Glue applied sparingly with a fine brush. Do one side; let it dry before turning to the other side.

4. *Optional:* Attach clip to a small clipboard and pad of note paper.

Fish Plaque

(See completed project on page 83.)

With a piece of leftover wood, you can make an unusual gift for a Pisces friend or for the hostess who invites you to her seashore home. This wooden fish could be used as an address plate, a cheese server, or a wall decoration.

Materials

wood, 12 inches × 20 inches × 1 inch
#220 sandpaper
drill (if you don't own one, borrow a friend's)
gesso or modeling paste
awl
household fork
acrylic paint in color of your choice (I used blue-green)
Liquid Pearl in color of your choice (again, I used blue-green)
turpentine
metallic wax (I used Treasure Jewels' "Green Amber" but could also have used Rub 'n Buff's "Grecian Gold" or Lustre Wax's green-gold shade)
Treasure Sealer or decoupage sealer
marine varnish

2 decorative hooks or cup hooks (optional)
chain to hang plaque (optional)
heavy cardboard (optional)
waxed paper or lint-free cloth (optional)

Procedure

1. Cut wood according to pattern, or have someone cut it for you. Sand well.
2. Drill a hole for the mouth of the fish 1½ inches in from the mouth indentation, as shown in the pattern.
3. Apply 2 thick coats of gesso or modeling paste over the front of the board for texture; allow drying time between coats. Apply 1 coat of gesso over the sides and the back of the board.
4. Use an awl to outline the fish scales and eye on the front of the board. See *Diagram A.* Use a fork to scratch in the tail and fins.
5. Apply 2 coats of acrylic paint to the board, allowing drying time between coats. As you paint the front, texturize each fish scale with curvy brush strokes; texturize the fish head by applying the paint with a patting motion of a sponge. Let dry.
6. Mix a small amount of Liquid Pearl with turpentine on a piece of aluminum foil, according to directions on the label. Flow mixture on the front and sides of the board. If the back will show when used, apply it to the back also.
7. Apply metallic wax to the front of the board, according to directions on the label. Rub off excess with a textured paper towel. Let it settle in grooves of scales and fins. Dampen a paper towel with turpentine and give it an additional wiping.
8. When dry, apply a coat of Treasure Sealer or decoupage sealer over the front of the board. Let dry.
9. Brush 2 coats of marine varnish over the entire board, allowing drying time between coats.
10. *Optional:* If you plan to hang the fish, attach 2 hooks and a chain to the top of the wood.
11. *Optional:* If you wish to print a name or address, use a stencil or trace letters or numbers; retrace onto heavy cardboard. Cut out numbers or letters with a sharp pair of pointed scissors. Paint the cutouts, including the edges, with acrylic paint in the color of your choice; let dry. Brush on a coat of marine varnish; let dry. Glue cutouts to the face of the board and press down; wipe off excess glue with a damp cloth. Cover with waxed paper or a lint-free cloth, place a weight on it, and let dry for 12 to 24 hours.

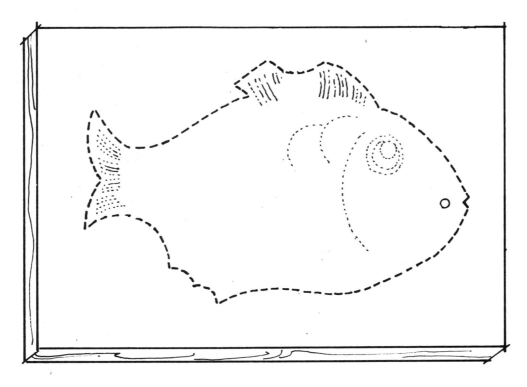

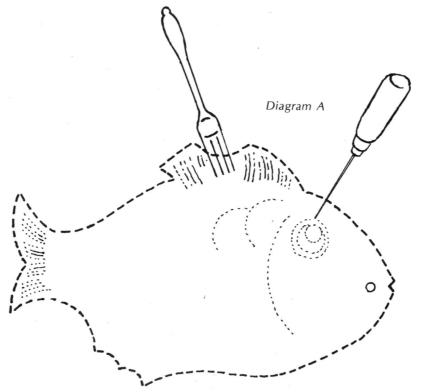

Diagram A

Tomato Basket Doll Cradle

(See completed project on page 7.)

A cardboard tomato basket (the kind thrown out by supermarkets or the kind you bring home from country roadside vegetable stands), leftover eyelet trim, scrap lumber, and remnants of dainty fabric—all can be combined to make a charming cradle for a little girl's doll.

Materials

cardboard tomato basket, 7½ inches × 15 inches, with wooden handle
gesso
#220 sandpaper
white quilted vinyl adhesive to line basket
instant decoupage (Fun Podge, Mod Podge, Decollage)
leftover fabric to cover basket outside (I used pink-and-white checked gingham)
waxed paper
brayer
wooden strip, ¼ inch × 10 inches × 5 inches
2 wooden strips, 1 inch × 9 inches × 2½ inches, shaped in a rocker curve
acrylic paint in color of your choice (I used white)
acrylic spray
Dow Corning Urethane Bond Glue

gathered eyelet ruffling (white) to go around top of basket
Velverette Craft Glue
velveteen ribbon, ¾ inch wide, to go around top edges of basket and to wind basket handle (I used pink)

Procedure

1. Inspect the tomato basket to make sure there are no breaks. Apply 1 coat of gesso to the outside of the basket to reinforce and to prevent the color of the grower's label from showing through the fabric. Allow to dry. Sand lightly.
2. Make a newspaper pattern for the 4 sides of the inside basket. Allow a ½-inch overlap at the bottom and a 1-inch overlap at the top; butt side seams. Cut out. Place newspaper pattern on vinyl adhesive and cut. Press adhesive-backed pieces into place, turning the top overlap to the outside of the basket and the bottom overlap to the inside bottom of the basket. Cut a newspaper pattern for the bottom of the basket. Cut vinyl according to the pattern; press in place on the inside basket bottom.
3. Apply instant decoupage over the outside of the basket. Let dry.
4. Brush a coat of instant decoupage over the fabric, keeping a piece of waxed paper underneath. Lift the fabric before it dries so that it does not stick to the waxed paper. When dry, turn the fabric and repeat the procedure on the other side; let dry. Your material will now cut easily and will not ravel.
5. Make a newspaper pattern for the outside of the basket; plan to cut the 2 long sides and the bottom in 1 piece of fabric, allowing a ½-inch turn-under seam allowance at the top and at the sides, on both sides of the basket. Cut out. Make a pattern to fit the 2 short sides of the basket, allowing a ½-inch turn-under seam on all 4 edges of each side. Cut out. Cut fabric according to patterns.
6. On the long piece of fabric, press under the top edge seam allowances and glue flat with instant decoupage. Apply a coat of instant decoupage to one of the long sides of the basket and to the back of the fabric that will cover that side. Glue the fabric to the basket; turn side seam allowances around the short side of the basket. Roll out excess glue and air bubbles with a brayer over a dampened paper towel. Continue in the same manner on the bottom of the basket and then onto the other long side.

7. Press under the seam allowance on all 4 edges of the short side pieces. Glue seam allowances flat with instant decoupage. Attach the side pieces in the same manner with instant decoupage. Let dry completely. Wash brayer well with soap and water when finished.

8. Apply a coat of instant decoupage over the basket outside. Let dry.

9. Sand wood pieces well. Nail the curved wooden strips *under the straight strip.*

10. Brush 2 coats of gesso over the wood, sanding between coats. Let dry.

11. Apply 2 coats of acrylic paint to wood, allowing drying time between coats.

12. Spray wood with 2 misty coats of acrylic spray, allowing drying time between coats.

13. Glue rocker construction to the bottom of the basket with Dow Corning Urethane Bond Glue. Let dry.

14. Glue eyelet ruffling around the outside top edge of the basket with Velverette Craft Glue. Glue velveteen ribbon around the outside top edge over the top of the eyelet ruffling.

15. Wind basket handle tightly with velveteen ribbon, applying a little glue at each end of the handle. Attach small velveteen bows, if you wish, to the ends of the handle on the outside of the basket and to one of short edges.

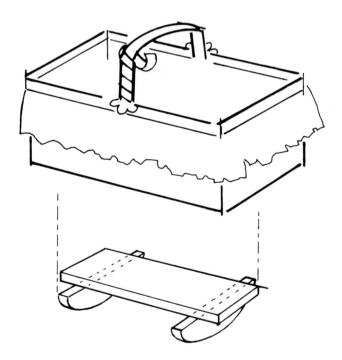

Golfer's Plaque
(See completed project on page 83.)

If you're not a golfer, you undoubtedly know one. At some time in your life I predict you'll need a gift idea for a friend who plays golf. You'll win your friend's heart with this message on a plaque: As part of my diet, I'm golfing everyday . . . my doctor told me to live on *GREENS* as much as possible.

Materials

distressed wood for plaque, size to fit printing and golf cutout (I used a 7- × 12-inch piece of wood; you can distress a piece of wood yourself or find it at sites of torn-down houses or buildings or buy it from a craft shop)

tools to distress wood: saw-toothed picture hanger, rasp, keys, chains, nails, hammer (optional: if necessary)

#220 and #400 sandpaper

stain of your choice

#0000 steel wool

black Stain-it (optional)

golf picture cut out from a sports magazine, greeting card, or gift wrapping paper

white acrylic paint (optional: to cover printing on back of magazine cutouts)

decoupage sealer

good grade parchment or white paper (I used a 4½- × 5½-inch piece)

India ink
cigarette
instant decoupage (Fun Podge, Mod Podge,
Decollage)
felt or wallpaper or gift wrapping paper to fit
back of plaque
decorative metal ring

Procedure

1. Distress wood, if not already distressed. Scratch wood with a saw-toothed hanger. Cut edges and make indentations with a rasp. Hammer and gouge with nails, keys, and chains.

2. Sand wood well, first using #220 sandpaper and ending with #400.

3. Apply stain to the wood, following directions on the label. Be sure to get stain into indentations; use a cotton swab to apply, if necessary. Rub off excess stain with steel wool.

4. *Optional:* Wipe edges of plaque with black Stain-it to give added depth and a finished border.

5. Cut out golf print. If printing appears on the back or if paper is thin, paint back with white acrylic paint so that printing or stain will not show through. Spray front of print with a coat of decoupage sealer.

6. On parchment or white paper, print by hand with pencil and then India ink: As part of my diet, I'm golfing everyday . . . my doctor told me to live on *GREENS* as much as possible. (Use a stencil or trace magazine letters if you don't print well. If you plan to make a number of plaques for a fundraiser project, ask someone on your committee who prints well to make a master copy; take to a printer and have copies made.) Spray printing with a coat of decoupage sealer when dry.

7. Rip excess paper from edges of printed message. Burn edges with a lit cigarette to give paper an aged look.

8. Apply a coat of instant decoupage to the front and back and edges of the plaque. Let dry. Apply another coat of instant decoupage to the front of the plaque.

9. Determine placement of cutout print and printing on the plaque. Coat back of golf print with instant decoupage; glue in place. Roll out excess glue and air bubbles with a brayer over a dampened paper towel. Roll from the center out to each of the 4 corners. If air bubbles develop, prick with a pin and roll again. Let dry.

10. Coat back of printed message with instant decoupage . Glue in place. Roll out with a brayer over a dampened paper towel. Let dry.

11. Apply another coat of instant decoupage over the front of the plaque as a protective finish. Let dry.

12. Cut felt to fit the back of the wood. Glue in place to prevent stain from bleeding through to the wall when hung.

13. Attach the saw-toothed metal hanger you used for distressing to the top center back of the plaque.

14. Attach a decorative metal ring to the center top edge of the plaque.

Bottle Vase with Stand

(See completed project on page 3.)

Bottle cutting is sweeping the country. Until this year, however, the only kind of bottle that could be cut was the perfectly round bottle. Now the company that manufactures Ephrem's Olde Time Bottle Cutter Kit has introduced an attachment that makes it possible to cut all shapes of bottles; the attachment is called Bottle Boss and will fit right on Ephrem's Olde Time Bottle Cutter. Here is a project calling for a square or rectangular bottle that is made into a lovely vase for flowers and greens.

Materials

square or rectangular liquor bottle: fifth, quart, or half gallon
support block
Bottle Boss
oil
candle
ice cubes
#220 and #400 sandpaper
polishing paper and powder (part of bottle cutting kit)
glass pie pan or piece of plate glass
epoxy glue

Procedure

1. Wash empty bottle well; soak off label.
2. Place the cutting wheel in the single hole on the right side of the Bottle Boss.
3. Place the center opening in the Bottle Boss on top of the wooden support block and tape in place, or place the opening on the neck of a circular bottle to give it support.
4. Pour a drop of oil over the cutting blade. Position the blade against the side of the square bottle, and rotate the bottle against the cutter. This will etch a cutting line around the sides of the bottle to be cut. Check to be sure there are no skips.
5. Holding the bottle horizontally, heat the etched line over the top of a candle flame, rotating the bottle slowly. Heat until the bottle is like a hot potato: not too hot to touch but too hot to hold.
6. Stand the bottle upright and rub an ice cube along the heated line until a crack develops. Do not force. If the bottle does not separate with a slight tug, reheat and cool again.
7. Polish both cut edges of the bottle with polishing paper and polishing powder.
8. Glue the bottom of the jar over the top with epoxy glue. Let glue dry thoroughly.

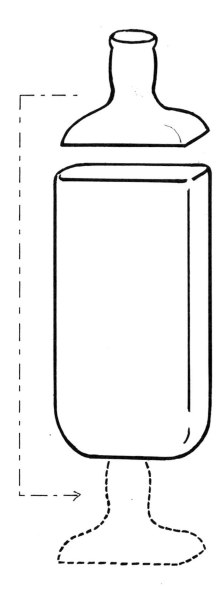

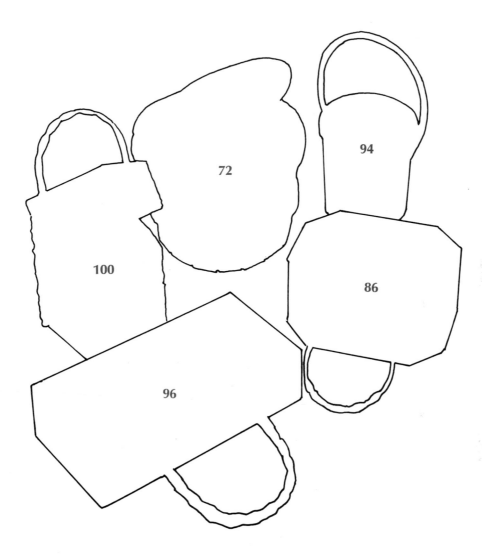

Details and instructions for projects shown may be found on page number indicated

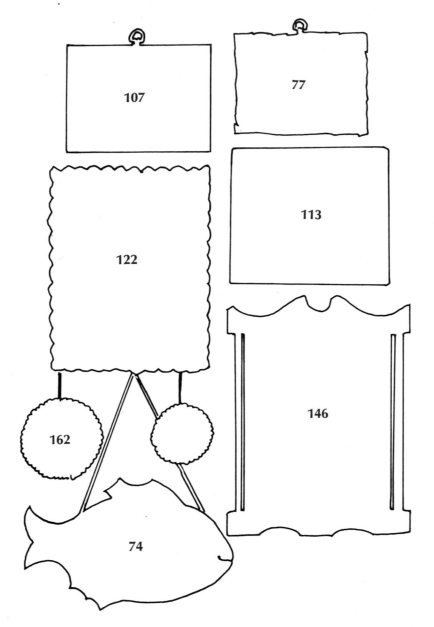

Details and instructions for projects shown may be found on page number indicated

Dear Nana, Please, Come Down.
Love
Cary

As part of my diet,
I'm golfing everyday.
My doctor told me to live
on GREENS
as much as possible.

18

U.S.
OPEN

WASTE
NOT.

WANT
NOT.

1818

P. S. Savannah

ABELL

Merry
Christmas!

Chapter
3

Personal Accessories and Family Mementos

Flashlight Lens Pendant
Shell Jewelry Dish
Seashell Pocketbook
Tea Strainer Sachet
Jewelry Box
Little Miss Pocketbook
Button 'n' Bead Bracelet
Wine Lover's Pocketbook
Paper Bag Wig Stand
Mother-of-Pearl Evening Bag
Repoussé Hand Mirror
Paint Bucket Curler Caddy
Immortalized Wedding Invitation
Man's Personalized Wastepaper Basket
Child's Drawing Plaque

Flashlight Lens Pendant

(See completed project on page 16.)

Before you throw away a broken flashlight, check the lens. If it isn't cracked, you have the makings of an elegant pendant that looks like a Victorian antique.

Materials

flashlight lens
vinegar
decoupage or manicure scissors
cutout from print of your choice
Decal-it
decoupage sealer
black acrylic spray paint
wooden circle: ⅜ inch thick, same diameter as lens, with a routed edge on one side
#220 sandpaper
stain or acrylic paint for wood in color of your choice
white glue
narrow gold cord braid to encircle lens (or gold metallic thread to crochet a cord)
small screw ring
gold chain (or metallic thread to crochet chain)

Procedure

1. Wash the glass lens with vinegar and water. Dry well, being careful to avoid leaving fingerprints on the glass.

2. With decoupage or manicure scissors, cut out designs from print of your choice. Keep the curved point of the scissors at a 45-degree angle, pointed away from the design. Hold your cutting hand still, except to open and close the scissor blades; with your other hand, feed the print into the scissor blades.

3. Apply a coat of Decal-it to the face of the cutout and to the underside of the glass lens, and press the print in place. Work out air bubbles and excess glue with your fingers on the underside of the lens. Remove excess Decal-it with a dampened sponge. Let dry.

4. Apply a coat of decoupage sealer over the underside of the lens to seal the print. Let dry.

5. Spray 2 misty coats of black paint to the underside of the lens, allowing drying time between coats. Let dry completely.

6. Sand all edges of the wooden circle well. Apply stain to both sides and edges of the wood, following directions on the product label. Wipe off excess stain with steel wool (or apply 2 coats of acrylic paint, allowing drying time between coats).

7. Glue glass lens to the flat side of the wood with white glue, adhering the underside of the lens to the flat side of the wood. The routed edge of the wood now becomes the back of the pendant.

8. Glue braid around the edges of the glass lens (or crochet gold metallic thread and glue on).

9. Insert a screw ring into the center top of the wood for hanging.

10. Put a chain (or crochet gold metallic thread to make a chain) through the screw ring to hang the pendant.

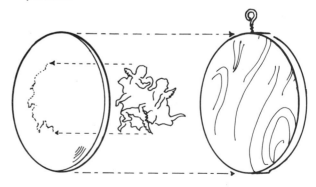

4. Glue pearls around the top outside edge of the shell, covering the fabric ends. Apply Velverette Craft Glue to one pearl at a time, as each one must be glued separately. With one hand, pick up the pearl with tweezers; with the other hand, use a brush to apply glue to the pearl. Set the pearl in place on the edge of the shell with your tweezers.

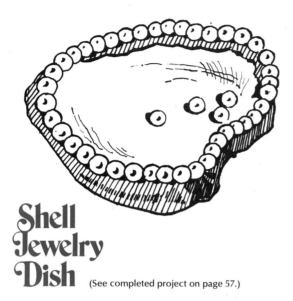

Shell Jewelry Dish

(See completed project on page 57.)

I rarely come back from a trip to the seashore without a collection of shells. I'm not alone, if the number of shells I've received from friends is any indication. Recently I was given a beautiful shell from Cape Cod. The inside was so pretty, I decided to use it as a guest room jewelry dish.

Materials

seashell of fairly good size
Velverette Craft Glue
lightweight rayon velvet, cut on bias, in color of your choice
pearls (use a broken strand of uniform-sized pearls or purchase in a craft store)
small brush

Procedure

1. Wash the shell with soap and water. Dry well.
2. Cover the back of the shell with glue.
3. While shell is wet with glue, pull bias-cut velvet over the back of the shell, bringing up to the top edge. Let dry. Carefully trim away excess fabric.

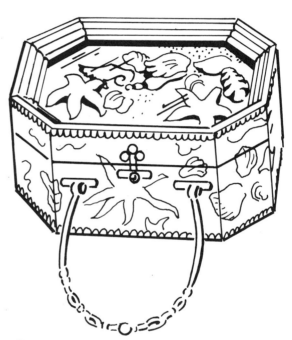

Seashell Pocketbook

(See completed project on page 80.)

Some gift wrapping papers are so beautiful that we don't have to be reminded not to throw them away. I received a gift wrapped in a paper printed with all kinds of seashells on a background of sand. I decided to make a pocketbook covered with the wrapping paper, using as my basic ingredient one of those wooden pocketbook boxes with a glass top shadow box lid. Inside the lid I put three-dimensional decoupage shells cut from the wrapping paper.

Materials

wooden pocketbook box with glass top shadow box lid (found in most craft stores)
#220 sandpaper
decoupage sealer
green acrylic paint
Treasure Jewels in green amber
tissue paper
gift wrapping paper
Plasti-tak
decoupage paste or white glue
brayer
gloss or semi-gloss instant spray finish
piece of very coarse sandpaper to fit base of shadow box
white glue
small seashells (optional)
decoupage or manicure scissors
Dow Corning Silicone Sealer
waxed paper
vinegar
old pair of clean cotton gloves
velveteen for lining in color of your choice
narrow gold metallic braid to go around the edges of the box 4 times
shirt cardboard
artfoam for side and bottom linings
Velverette Craft Glue
awl
pocketbook hinges, catch, handle, and handle hardware
4 decorative ball feet

Procedure

1. Sand well all edges of the wooden box and lid.
2. Cover all surfaces of the box with decoupage sealer. Let dry thoroughly. Lightly sand again.
3. Brush 2 coats of acrylic paint over all surfaces of the box that you do not expect to cover with gift wrapping paper. (This will include the outside lid molding, all areas inside and outside the shadow box, and the inside top and bottom lip edges of the box.) Allow drying time between coats.
4. Apply Treasure Jewels over the painted areas for a metallic look. Buff with a soft cloth.
5. Press tissue paper against each outside section of the box lid and bottom to make a pattern for cutting out the wrapping paper. (The tissue paper will enable you to see through to the wrapping paper so that you can match patterns.) Cut out tissue paper patterns.
6. Place pattern on gift wrapping paper. Match each section, both side seams and lid opening seams. Cut out gift wrapping paper.
7. Spray the paper with 3 misty coats of decoupage sealer after it is cut. (Do not spray before cutting; cutting breaks the seal.)
8. Use Plasti-tak to place each section of paper on the box. Before gluing, be sure the pieces match at the seams.
9. Glue paper to the box, one section at a time, with decoupage paste or white glue. Roll out air bubbles and excess glue with a brayer, rolling from the center to each of the 4 corners, before going on to the next section. (You may roll over a very slightly dampened paper towel, but be careful—moisture could make the print run.) Wipe off excess glue and allow to dry overnight.
10. Spray all paper-covered and painted surfaces, inside and outside, with 4 or 5 very misty coats of instant spray finish (heavy coats will run).
11. Press down aluminum foil to shape the pattern of the bottom piece of wood that forms the base of the shadow box. Cut out the foil; use it as a pattern to cut a piece of coarse sandpaper. Glue sandpaper to the wood with white glue.
12. If you have a collection of beautiful seashells, glue the shells at random on the sandpaper, or cut out the shells from the gift wrapping paper, as I did, and attach them in a three-dimensional technique. Using decoupage or manicure scissors, cut out an assortment of shells. Keep the curved point of the scissors pointed away from the print at a 45-degree angle. Hold your cutting hand still except to open and close the scissor blades; with your other hand, feed the paper into the scissor blades.
13. Shape the shells—the pictures on the wrapping paper will help you determine which part of the shell needs shaping. Most of the shells curve outward; hold these in the palm of your hand, face down. Using the back of a small spoon, the eraser end of a pencil, the smooth end of your burnisher, or the flat of your index fingernail, gently press the piece down into the palm of your hand.
14. Spray shaped shells with 2 very misty coats of spray finish. Let dry.
15. Plan placement of shell cutouts on sandpaper, according to the diagram. Working on one shell at a time, squeeze out a little silicone sealer to the back of a shell, pulling the tube away so that the

glue remaining resembles the peak of a beaten egg white. Use tweezers to help you pick up and place shells. Set the pieces down carefully to adhere them to the sandpaper. To apply sealer to tiny shell cutouts, squeeze out sealer onto waxed paper and apply small amounts to the tiny shell with a toothpick. Pull into an erect position any shells you might have flattened while gluing. Pick up excess adhesive with a toothpick immediately. Let dry.

16. Wash glass top with vinegar and water. Dry well. Handle with a pair of clean cotton gloves to eliminate fingermarks. Glue glass top to the inside of the box lid.

17. Glue the shadow box bottom, with its shell arrangement, in place on the bottom of the lid. Allow to dry thoroughly.

18. Make an aluminum foil pattern for the box lid; press an indentation into the foil at the edge of the glued shadow box. Cut foil. Cut velveteen according to the foil pattern. Do not turn under edges of fabric; glue cut velveteen flat to the bottom of the shadow box on the lid. Glue gold metallic braid to cover the cut edges of the velveteen.

19. Make an aluminum foil pattern for each inside section on the sides of the bottom of the purse. Cut foil. Cut cardboard sections slightly smaller than the foil patterns. Mark sections "front" and "back" and number each piece so that you know where it belongs in the final assembling. Cut artfoam, using each section of cardboard as a pattern, to add a puffy, elegant look to the lining. Glue artfoam to back of cardboard sections.

20. Place velveteen right side down on a cutting surface. Line up cardboard sections on top of the fabric in the order in which they will be glued to the box sides, allowing a small area in between each cardboard seam. Cut velveteen in one continuous piece, allowing a ½-inch turnover at the top edge, a 1-inch extra allowance at the bottom, and an extra ¼ inch at each of the end seams.

21. Glue the ½-inch turnover to the back of the cardboard at the top seam with Velverette Craft Glue; glue the ¼-inch turnover to the back of the cardboard at the end seams.

22. Place the lining inside the box to check fit. When satisfied with the fit, remove the lining, apply Velverette Craft Glue to cardboard backing, and glue the lining in place. Push the end seams into a corner that will not be obvious when the purse is opened. Let the 1-inch overlap at the bottom remain unglued. It will be attached when the purse bottom lining is glued in.

23. Make an aluminum foil pattern for the inside bottom lining of the box. Cut foil. Cut cardboard slightly smaller than the foil pattern. Cut a piece of artfoam the same size as the cardboard. Glue the artfoam to the cardboard.

24. Cut velveteen according to the cardboard pattern, allowing an extra ½ inch on all edges. Glue the velveteen to the back of the cardboard on the ½-inch turnover edges only. Check fit; if satisfied, let glue dry. Check fit again. Apply glue to the cardboard and attach the lining to the bottom of the purse. (The 1-inch overlap on the side linings will now be secured under the bottom lining.)

25. Glue metallic braid around the edges where the side and bottom linings meet at the bottom of the box.

26. Glue braid around the outside top lid edge of the box and the outside bottom edge.

27. Place the top and bottom of the box together and hold in position with rubber bands. Measure carefully to place hinges on the back edges equally distant from the ends of the box. Mark placement of screw holes with a pencil. Remove the hinges; start holes for screws with an awl. Place the hinges again; set in screws about halfway and then go back and tighten screws. Remove rubber bands.

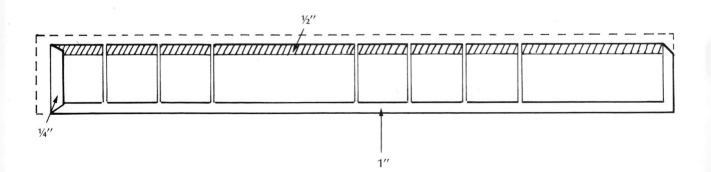

28. Measure carefully to find midway point between the ends of the front. Place the catch, mark screw holes, and proceed as with the hinges.

29. Attach handle in the same manner, measuring equal distances from the ends of the box for the placement of handle hardware. Use the same technique for attaching the hardware screws.

30. Attach decorative ball feet to the bottom of the box, one at each of the 4 corners, to protect the finish.

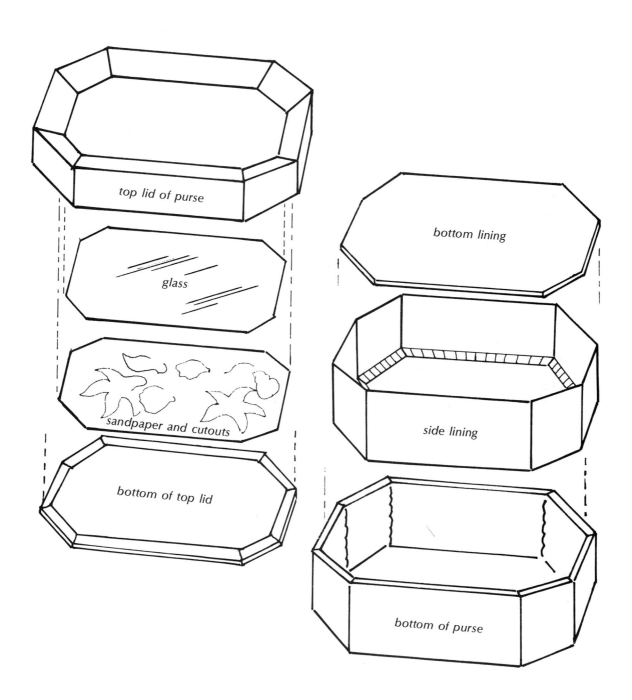

top lid of purse

glass

sandpaper and cutouts

bottom of top lid

bottom lining

side lining

bottom of purse

Tea Strainer Sachet

(See completed project on page 16.)

Don't throw away acorn-shaped tea strainers when they get discolored or slightly dented. Paint and decorate them and then fill with your favorite scent in the form of ready-made sachets or a potpourri of dried flowers, herbs, or spices. When hung in the closet, this sachet will keep your clothes smelling fresh for a long time.

Materials

1 large and 2 small acorn-shaped tea strainers with screw-on tops
acrylic spray paint in color of your choice
spray finish
Velverette Craft Glue
several yards of narrow velvet ribbon in color of your choice
bunch of tiny velvet forget-me-nots in color of your choice
4 mm. pearls or beads of your choice (you may use a broken necklace)
three small sachets in scent of your choice or a potpourri of dried flowers, herbs, or spices (enough to fill strainers)

Procedure

1. Cut the chain attached to the large tea strainer to a length of 4½ inches. Cut the chain attached to each small tea strainer to a length of 1½ inches. Attach one of the short chains to a link 1 inch from the top of the 4½-inch chain; attach the other short chain to a link 2½ inches from the top of the 4½-inch chain.
2. Spray the strainers, lids, and chains with 2 misty coats of acrylic paint, being careful not to clog the holes in the strainers with paint. Let dry.
3. Apply 2 misty coats of spray finish, allowing drying time between coats.
4. Glue 2 rows of ribbon, one overlapping the other, around the edges of the strainer lids.
5. Separate the flowers and cut off stems. Glue individual flowers around the edges of the lids on top of the ribbon.
6. Glue pearls or beads to the top of the strainer lids. Let dry.
7. Fill strainers with sachets or potpourri. Screw the lids on strainers.
8. Make streamers of velvet ribbon cut 12 inches long (or as long as you need for hanging). Insert ribbon through a link in the long chain; make a loop bow at the top.

Jewelry Box (See completed project on page 16.)

Don't throw away an old wooden silver chest. Reverse the lid and use it as a shadow box to frame a three-dimensional floral picture. Paint the box, line it with a leftover piece of velveteen, and your old silver chest can become a beautiful, unusual box for jewelry.

Materials

old wooden silver chest or any similar wooden box with a lid
#220 and #400 sandpaper
wood putty (optional: to repair damaged parts of box)
gesso
acrylic paint in color of your choice
antiquing glaze
varnish
shirt cardboard
velveteen lining fabric, ¼ to ½ yard, depending on box size (if you have a piece of leftover velvet, use it; if not, look for a remnant)
white glue
braided trim, to go around edges of velveteen, in same color

2 or more duplicate floral prints, depending on box size (I've chosen flowers from a store shopping bag)
decoupage sealer
decoupage or manicure scissors
Dow Corning Silicone Sealer
Velverette Craft Glue
glass to fit top of lid
vinegar
old pair of clean cotton gloves
gold decoupage braid to go around edges of glass
awl

Procedure

1. Remove hinges, catch, and feet from box. Sand thoroughly. Fill in any damaged area and holes with wood putty. Sand again.

2. Brush a coat of gesso over the outside of the box, the inside opening edges of the lid, and the box bottom. Let dry. Sand. Apply another coat of gesso.

3. Brush on 2 coats of acrylic paint if you are using a dark color, 3 coats if using a pastel shade. Allow adequate drying time and sand with #400 sandpaper between coats.

4. Apply antiquing glaze, according to directions on the label. Wipe off excess with a textured paper towel. Allow to dry overnight.

5. Apply 3 coats of clear varnish, allowing drying time between coats. Let dry thoroughly.

6. To get lining patterns for the inside of the box, press one continuous piece of aluminum foil against the sides of the box and then fit a piece of foil into the bottom of box. Cut foil. Next, cut 4 cardboard pieces for the sides according to your foil pattern, following indentation marks in foil. Trim ¼ inch from the top and bottom edges of the cardboard to allow for the width of the fabric turn-under (you will be fitting the sides flush into the side corners and not turning under the fabric at these corners). Then cut cardboard for the bottom lining according to your foil pattern, less ¼ inch on all edges. Follow the same procedure to obtain a cardboard lining for the sides and bottom of the lid.

7. Cut velveteen lining for the 4 sides of the box, according to your cardboard pieces, plus ½ inch on the top and bottom edges for fabric turn-under. Cut the side corner seams flush with the cardboard sides. Cut lining for the bottom of the box according to cardboard piece, plus a ½-inch turn-under on all edges. Cut linings for the box lid in the same manner.

8. Thin white glue with water. Working on waxed paper, glue the ½-inch turn-under at the top and bottom edges of the velveteen side linings to the cardboard on the reverse side. Glue the ½-inch turn-under allowances on all 4 edges of the bottom linings to the reverse side of the cardboard. Be careful not to get glue on velveteen as it's impossible to remove. Use a small brush to spread the glue. Apply glue lightly so that it does not soak through fabric and stain it. Check to see whether pieces fit before allowing the glue to dry. If pieces are too tight, trim cardboard and reglue. Let all fabric-covered pieces dry overnight. Check fitting again and make final adjustments. Glue finished pieces into the box and lid, gluing the side linings first and the bottom linings last.

9. Study your prints carefully before you begin to work with them. One print will be a background print; the other, a cutting print. However, unlike most dimensional decoupage projects in which the background print is not cut, you will cut all background material from your flower in the background print. Determine which parts of the flowers and leaves in your cutting print you wish to feature. These should be the parts of a flower or leaf that seem to come toward you as you look at them. Decide whether these parts would naturally curve in an inward or outward direction.

10. Spray the backs of both prints with 3 misty coats of decoupage sealer to make cutting easier.

11. Using decoupage or manicure scissors, cut away all background material from the background print. Cut out the pieces you plan to feature from your cutting print, doing large flowers first, smaller flowers and petals next, and foliage last. Assemble cutting print pieces on a piece of waxed paper as you will place them on the background print. Cut with the curved point of the scissors pointed away from the print at a 45-degree angle. Hold your cutting hand still, except to open and close the scissor blades; with your other hand, feed the print into the scissor blades. Cut the inside areas of the print first; cut the outside areas later.

12. Contour or shape your cutouts as closely to their three-dimensional shape as possible. If they should curve inward (concave), hold them in the palm of your hand face up; if they should curve outward (convex), hold them face down. To shape them, use the back of a small spoon, the eraser end of a pencil, or the flat of your index fingernail.

Gently press the piece down into the palm of your hand to give it the shape you desire. Round edges of petals.

13. Work on one piece at a time in assembling cutout pieces. Be careful of handling cutouts after they are shaped. Squeeze out a little silicone sealer to the back of a cutout, pulling the tube away so that the remaining glue resembles the peak of a beaten egg white. Use tweezers to help you pick up and place pieces. To apply sealer to tiny pieces, squeeze out some onto waxed paper and apply with a toothpick.

14. Place the cutout over its duplicate area on the background print. Set down carefully so that it will adhere to the background print. Pull up any flowers or leaves you might have flattened in gluing. Pick up excess adhesive with a toothpick immediately, and remove as quickly as possible any smudges of adhesive on your background print with a damp paper towel. Continue placing the cutouts, one at a time, until your three-dimensional decoupage is completed.

15. Measure the finished three-dimensional print and measure the box lid to center the print on the velvet lining. Lightly mark your measurements on the lining. Carefully turn the print to the wrong side and apply Velverette Craft Glue. Glue braided trim around lining. Gently place the glued side of the print down on the marked area of the box lid lining. Allow to dry overnight.

16. Wash the glass for the top of the reversed lid in a solution of vinegar and water; clean thoroughly and dry well. Handle glass with an old pair of clean cotton gloves to keep fingerprints from the surface. Using a brush, lightly apply white glue (or epoxy glue, if you wish) to the edges of the lid. Allow the glue to set for a moment, gently place the glass over the glued area, and press down carefully. Let dry.

17. *Optional:* Spray gold braid with 3 misty coats of decoupage sealer to protect the gold color, allowing drying time between coats. Wipe with antiquing glaze; wipe off excess glaze with a textured paper towel. Let dry completely. Apply 2 more coats of decoupage sealer to protect the antiquing. When dry, place braid face down on waxed paper. Lightly apply white glue to the back of the braid; allow to set until it becomes sticky. Glue the braid to the edge of the glass on all 4 sides, letting half of the braid overlap the side edges. Mitre corners.

18. Apply a coat of antiquing glaze to the hinges, catch, and feet. Wipe off excess with a paper towel; let dry. Varnish; let dry.

19. Place the lid and the box together, with lid in reversed position, of course; hold in position with rubber bands. Measure carefully to place hinges on the back edges equally distant from the ends of the box. Mark screw holes with a pencil; remove the hinges. Start holes for screws with an awl. Place the hinges again; set in screws about halfway and then go back and tighten screws. Remove rubber bands.

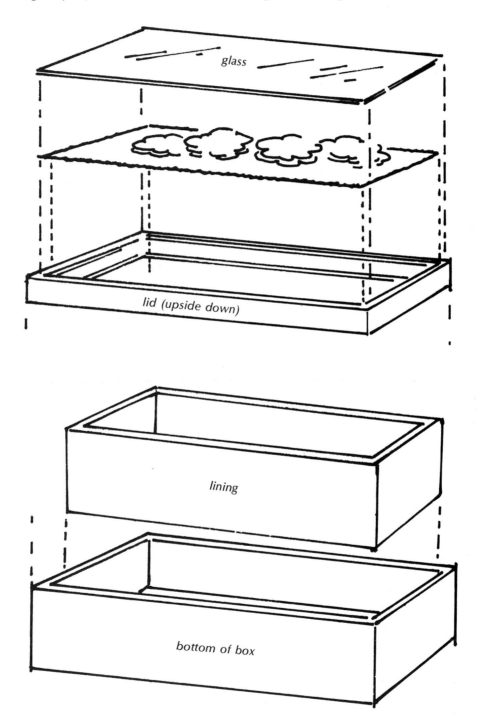

glass

lid (upside down)

lining

bottom of box

Little Miss Pocketbook

(See completed project on page 80.)

A clear plastic food container, some gift wrapping paper, an old pocketbook handle, and some leftover fabric produce an absolutely charming pocketbook for a favorite little girl.

Materials

clear hard plastic food storage container: 1-quart size in circular shape
vinegar
decoupage or manicure scissors
juvenile gift wrapping paper
Plasti-tak
Decal-it
decoupage sealer
acrylic paint in color of your choice
flexible old pocketbook handle in compatible color (or handle that can be painted)
hardware to attach pocketbook handle
shirt cardboard
leftover fabric for lining
white glue
decorative edging to go around outside lid edge

Procedure

1. Wash container with vinegar and water. Dry well.

2. With decoupage or manicure scissors, cut out designs from gift wrapping paper. Keep the curved point of the scissors pointed away from the design at a 45-degree angle. Hold your cutting hand still except to open and close scissor blades; with your other hand, feed picture into scissor blades.

3. Plan placement of cutouts around the inside of the container lid. Use Plasti-tak to place the cutouts until you are satisfied with your composition. Remove the Plasti-tak on each piece, one at a time, before you attach the cutout permanently.

4. Apply a coat of Decal-it to the face of each cutout and to the area inside the container and the lid where the cutout will be attached. Press the cutouts in place. Work out air bubbles and excess glue with your fingers. Remove the remaining Decal-it with a dampened sponge. Let dry.

5. Apply a coat of decoupage sealer over the back of the glued cutouts to seal them. Let dry.

6. Paint the inside of the container and the inside top of the lid with 2 coats of acrylic paint, allowing drying time between coats. Do not paint the inside lid edge; let it remain clear.

7. Attach the pocketbook handle. Make a hole 1½ inches down from the top on either side of the plastic container to attach the hardware that will secure the handle. Use a heated awl or ice pick to make the necessary holes. Attach handle to the outside of the purse.

8. Press aluminum foil into the container bottom, around the container sides in one piece, and into the inside top of the lid to make 3 lining patterns. Cut foil. Cut cardboard according to the patterns, trimming each edge of the cardboard slightly to allow for fabric overlap.

9. Cut fabric according to the cardboard patterns, adding a ½-inch turn-under on all edges of the side piece and a ¼-inch turn-under on the 2 circular pieces.

10. Attach fabric to the cardboard pieces, gluing only the turned-under edges on the reverse side of the cardboard. Check for fit before letting dry. Trim edges of cardboard and reglue if lining does not lie flat.

11. Spread glue on the inside container sides. Attach the fabric-covered cardboard side piece first. Overlap and glue the edges where the seams meet. Spread glue on the bottom of the container inside; glue the bottom circle in place. Glue the lid circle in place. (This method of lining makes it easy to replace a lining that becomes soiled.)

12. Glue decorative edging around outside lid edge.

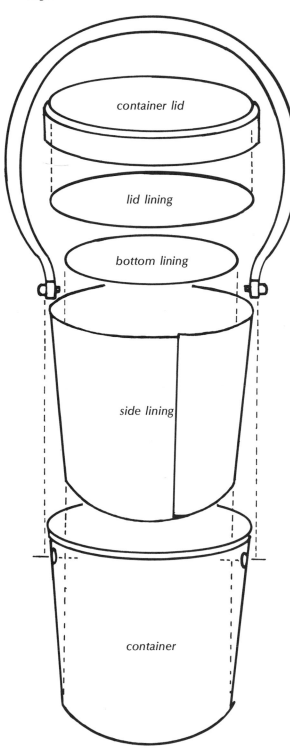

container lid

lid lining

bottom lining

side lining

container

Button'n'Bead Bracelet

(See completed project on page 16.)

Would you believe an attractive new bracelet might be no farther away than your sewing box? For the person who can't crochet and would like to make crocheted-looking costume jewelry, this is the answer. Stitch old buttons and beads onto a piece of elastic, stitch the elastic ends together, and behold —a new bracelet.

Go through a box of your old buttons, or ask an older relative if you may look through hers. The older buttons really are the prettier ones for this project.

Materials

2-inch-wide elastic band to go around wrist plus 1 inch extra or stretch band material used for waistbands in slacks, etc.
old buttons and beads

Procedure

1. Cut elastic to size. Overlap ends ½ inch; sew ends together.
2. Plan placement of buttons and beads on elastic, using colors and designs to best advantage. Sew buttons and beads in place.

Wine Lover's Pocketbook

(See completed project on page 80.)

Many times we learn more from our mistakes than we do from our successes. One of the prettiest pocketbooks ever made in our shop was the result of a mistake.

Some friends of mine collected many mementos as they traveled through three continents. Among them were the labels from wine and mineral water bottles.

They decided to use the labels on a wooden box to make a decoupaged pocketbook. After carefully applying ten coats of varnish, suddenly, for no reason we could understand, the finish cracked. They began work on another box, and I suggested that this time they allow double the drying time between coats of finish. Once again, after ten coats of varnish, tiny cracks appeared all over the finish. Since the cracks were beyond repair, we decided to make them more obvious with Decal-it, Crackle-it, and Age-it. This worked successfully so that now they have two finished boxes with an aged, antiqued look.

We learned two lessons from this mishap. Bottle labels, stamps, and some greeting cards and prints have waxed finishes that reject other finishes and varnishes. If you do not want the cracked look, be sure to soak them well in hot water and seal the prints thoroughly before you work with them. If you should, however, have a mishap, accept it and work with it.

Materials

wooden pocketbook box (available in craft or department stores)
#220 and #400 sandpaper
gesso
acrylic paint in color of your choice
wine bottle labels or labels of choice, approximately 14
decoupage sealer
Plasti-tak
decoupage paste or white glue
brayer
Decal-it*
Crackle-it*
Age-it*
lacquer or varnish of your choice
#0000 steel wool
decoupage wax
small piece of felt (could be from man's old hat)
adhesive paper with burlap texture to line box
gold metallic braid to go around opening inside edges of lid and box bottom
awl
pocketbook hinges, catch, handle, and handle hardware

* These products are available together in a kit, or they may be purchased separately.

Procedure

1. Sand wooden box well inside and outside, starting with #220 sandpaper and ending with #400.
2. Brush gesso inside and outside box to strengthen the wood. Let dry.
3. Apply 2 coats of acrylic paint over the outside of the box and along the inside edges, allowing adequate drying time between coats. Sand lightly.
4. Soak wine labels in hot water to remove wax finish. Let dry.
5. Seal labels with 3 misty coats of decoupage sealer, allowing adequate drying time between coats. Let dry completely.
6. Plan composition of labels on the pocketbook. Use Plasti-tak to place them until you are satisfied with composition. With a light pencil mark, mark placement of each label as you remove it for gluing.

7. Wet back of label with water before beginning to paste. Glue down labels one at a time with decoupage paste or white glue. Work on one side of the box at a time. As a side is glued, cover with a slightly dampened paper towel and roll out excess glue and air bubbles with a brayer. Roll from the center to each of the 4 corners. If air bubbles develop, prick with a pin and roll again. Wipe off any paste residue on the labels. Continue until all sides of the lid and box bottom are covered. Let dry overnight.

8. Apply 2 coats of Decal-it over the outside sections of the box, allowing drying time between coats. Let dry completely.

9. Flow on a generous coating of Crackle-it for bold cracks or a thin coat for small cracks. Brush out. Dry without heat or hot air.

10. When dry, squeeze a teaspoonful of Age-it onto a paper towel or piece of cheesecloth. Wipe on and let set for a few minutes; wipe off with a clean paper towel or cloth and let dry from 12 to 24 hours.

11. When thoroughly dry, apply your first coat of lacquer or varnish, following directions for application on the label. Be sure to apply finish to all inside edges of the box. Apply at least 10 coats before sanding. Cure overnight before the first sanding, longer if the weather is humid.

12. Wrap a piece of #400 sandpaper over the padded side of your sanding block. Wet sandpaper with soap suds, and sand in a circular motion over all areas of the box. When sides feel smooth, dry with a lint-free rag or paper towel.

13. Continue to apply additional coats of finish until the labels are completely submerged. Wet the sandpaper again, and repeat the sanding procedure as directed. Dry well.

14. With #0000 steel wool, gently polish the sections of the box in a straight up and down motion to eliminate sandpaper scratches. The more you polish, the prettier the finish will become. Wipe with a lint-free cloth. Set aside to cure for 2 weeks.

15. Apply a light coat of decoupage wax over the sections of the box. Using a small piece of felt, polish in a circular motion.

16. Make an aluminum foil pattern for the 4 sides of the inside box bottom. Allow a ½-inch overlap at the bottom; butt the side seams. Cut foil. Place the foil pattern on adhesive paper and cut out lining. Press adhesive-backed pieces into place, turning the bottom overlap onto the inside bottom of the box.

17. Cut a foil pattern for the bottom of the box. Cut adhesive paper according to the pattern; press in place on the box bottom. Repeat the same procedure for the lid of the box.

18. Glue gold metallic braid at the edge of the lining around the opening inside edges of the lid and box bottom.

19. Place the top and bottom of the box together; hold in position with rubber bands. Measure carefully to place hinges on the back edges equally distant from the ends of the box. Mark screw holes with a pencil and remove hinges. Start holes for screws with an awl. Place the hinges again; set in screws about halfway and then go back and tighten screws. Remove rubber bands.

20. Measure carefully to place the catch midway between the ends of the front of the box. Mark screw holes. Proceed as with the hinges.

21. Attach handle in the same manner, measuring equal distances from the ends of the box for the placement of handle hardware. (If you do not have special hardware, you can screw in 2 cup hooks, tightening them as you attach the handle.)

VARIATION 1: Decoupage a desk box with labels. Omit handle or catch.

VARIATION 2: Decoupage a wooden serving tray in the same way.

98

Paper Bag Wig Stand

(See completed project on page 16.)

Don't throw away a brown paper bag, colored tissue paper, or a wooden dowel (possibly the handle of a child's outgrown push-toy). You can use them to make a delightful wig stand that looks good even without a wig.

Materials

2 Styrofoam balls: one, 6 inches in diameter, and the other, 5 inches

gesso

wooden dowel stick, 10 inches long (or whatever length suits your needs) and ¾ inch in diameter

masking tape

large brown paper bag, supermarket type

Drape-it (the best product to work with for draping and shaping fabric or paper; if not available, mix wallpaper paste and white glue)

T-straight pins

instant decoupage (Fun Podge, Mod Podge, Decollage)

colored tissue paper

acrylic paint: white, brown, and red

clear acrylic spray

2 yards velveteen ribbon, 1 inch wide

Procedure

1. Cut 6-inch Styrofoam ball in half.

2. Apply a coat of gesso over the 5-inch ball and over one of the pieces of the 6-inch ball. (Don't throw the other half away; save it for something else.)

3. Find the centers of the Styrofoam balls to insert the wooden dowel. (It is essential to locate the exact center; otherwise, the stand will be off balance and will fall over.) Divide the 5-inch ball in half by placing a piece of masking tape across the outside circumference. Do the same with the half ball. Divide each into quarters by wrapping another piece of masking tape across the outside circumference. The point at which the 2 pieces of tape cross one another is the center of the ball. You will have a top and bottom centerpoint on the 5-inch ball; you will have only a top center point on the cut 6-inch ball.

4. With a pencil, start a hole in the center of the 6-inch half ball. Push the wooden dowel into the center of the hole about 2 inches deep. Remove the dowel carefully so as not to increase the size of the hole. Put glue into the hole and insert the dowel again. Let glue dry completely before continuing your work so that you will not dislodge the dowel.

5. Start a hole in the center bottom of the 5-inch ball with a pencil. Insert the dowel 2 inches up into the ball. Remove dowel carefully, put glue into the hole, insert the dowel again, and let dry completely.

6. Cut 2 circles from the paper bag, each large enough to cover one half of the 5-inch ball.

7. Pour Drape-it into a container (or mix wallpaper paste according to directions on the package and add glue to the mixture). Dip the circles into mixture. Place one circle around the front half of the ball; hold in place at the edges with T-straight pins. Place the other circle around the back of the ball; remove one at a time the T-straight pins holding the first circle, and use them to hold both circles in place at the seam. Trim rough edges of paper, if there are any.

8. While the circles are still wet, use the eraser end of a pencil to push up on the front center of the ball, making an indentation and then a slight raise in the paper to shape a nose. Let circles dry completely; remove T-straight pins when dry.

9. Cut the rest of the brown paper bag into strips measuring from 2 to 6 inches wide and 12 to 20 inches long. Fold strips lengthwise into 3 sections, folding raw edges to the inside. See *Diagram A.*

10. Dip the strips into Drape-it (or the wallpaper paste and glue mixture). Run the strips vertically through your fingers to remove excess Drape-it, wrinkling the paper as you handle it to achieve the textured look of hair.

11. Decide where you wish the hair part on your wig stand head to be and plan the hairdo. Think of the strips of paper as sections of hair. You will be pinch-creasing each paper strip at its center and attaching it to the wig stand with T-straight pins at the part line; one part of the strip will hang to the right of the part, the other part of the strip to the left. See *Diagram B.* Begin at the front and work toward the back; overlap strips at the part line as you add each section. With your fingers, mold and shape waves and swirls into the sections of paper, just as you would shape a hair style.

12. Form 3 of the longer strips into a raised swirl toward the back of the wig stand head. Hold in place with T-straight pins at the place where the swirl twists. Let strips air-dry. Remove pins when the strips are almost dry, and then let stand overnight.

13. Apply a coat of instant decoupage to the dowel and to the bottom half-circle base of the stand. Let dry.

14. Brush on another coat of instant decoupage over the same areas. Tear tissue paper into small pieces; place pieces on top of the wet dowel and ball base until the entire surfaces are covered. Pat down the pieces with your brush. When the tissue has dried, repeat the same procedure over the bottom flat side of the base. Prop the side so that the bottom base can dry.

15. Apply another coat of instant decoupage over the tissue-covered surfaces. Allow to dry completely for 24 hours or longer.

16. Frost hair on wig stand by dry-brushing the hair with white paint. Dip your brush into the paint; remove most of the paint from the brush against the side of the jar or by brushing back and forth on scrap paper until very little paint remains on the brush and you begin to get a streaky look. Dry-brush white paint at various places on the brown paper strips.

17. Paint on facial features; see *Diagram C.* Paint eyes, eyebrows, lashes, and beauty mark dark brown. Paint a white spot on the eyes. Paint the lips red. Let dry for 48 hours.

18. Spray entire wig stand with several misty coats of clear acrylic spray, allowing drying time between coats.

19. Tie velveteen ribbon around the neck of the wig stand, letting each side of the knotted ribbon hang down as a streamer. Cut an inverted V into the ribbon ends. Make 2 velvet bows, cutting inverted V's into the ends. Glue one at the neck; glue the other at the front part line of the hairdo.

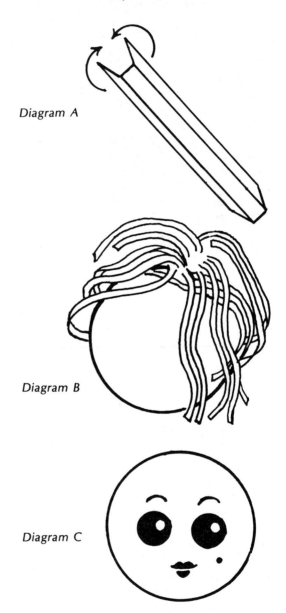

Diagram A

Diagram B

Diagram C

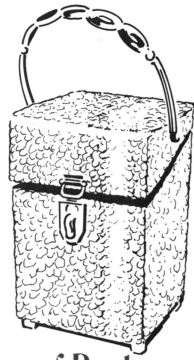

Mother-of-Pearl Evening Bag

(See completed project on page 80.)

Don't throw away any unusual cigar boxes. Some of them may make striking handbags. For this pearl evening bag, I found a narrow, deep box with a flip-up lid. I lined it with a piece of pink velveteen from an old party dress; your lining can be a piece of leftover brocade, velvet, or tapestry. I chose a gold handle, gold hinges, and a matching purse catch. If you have a lovely necklace that's broken, it might make an attractive handle.

Materials

wooden cigar box or wooden pocketbook box
#220 and #400 sandpaper
gesso
natural pearl paint (if not available, use an
    acrylic base paint in color of your choice)
lacquer thinner
white glue
pearl flakes
narrow gold decoupage braid to go around the
    box 4 times
waxed paper
burnisher
decoupage sealer
lacquer finish of your choice (such as Coat
    Royale or Fun Finish)
#0000 steel wool
shirt cardboard
lining fabric, ¼ to ½ yard, depending on box size
small piece of foam shipping material or artfoam
    (optional)
pocketbook hinges, catch, handle, and hardware
    (or an old necklace and 2 screw-in eye
    hooks)
4 decorative metal ball feet

Procedure

1. Remove all labels and hardware from the box. Sand well.
2. Brush 2 coats of gesso on the outside of the box and on the inside edges, sanding and allowing adequate drying time between coats.
3. Stir bottle of natural pearl paint well. Brush thin coat over box outside and on inside edges, according to directions on the label. Let dry. Brush on a second, heavier coat, brushing in the same direction. Clean brush immediately after use with lacquer thinner.
4. Spread glue on a small area of the box at a time. Sprinkle pearl flakes over the glued area. Let dry. Tap slightly to remove excess flakes, and save the flakes to use over again. If an area is uncovered, apply more glue and add more pearl flakes. (Be careful not to get flakes on the inside edges of the box or it will not close.) Continue until one side is covered. Let side dry completely before turning to another side so that flakes won't fall off. When dry, turn and continue to work on small areas at a time until all sides of the box and lid are covered. Let dry 24 hours.
5. Sand lightly and carefully with #400 sandpaper.
6. Place the decoupage braid face down on waxed paper. Lightly brush glue on the back; allow to set until it becomes sticky. Glue braid around the top and bottom edges of the lid and the box bottom. Press the braid down with the wide edge of a burnisher. Wipe off excess glue.

7. Spray 2 misty coats of decoupage sealer over the outside of the box, allowing drying time between coats. Let dry.

8. Flow on lacquer over each side of the box. Stir lacquer well in a figure-eight motion so as not to create bubbles. Dip brush in lacquer; do not wipe off excess on the edge of the can. Paint with a broad stroke, going from one side to the other. Dip again and repeat until the sides are covered. Be sure to apply finish to all inside edges of the box. Let dry completely before applying second coat. Continue applying subsequent coats of lacquer in the same manner. Apply at least 6 coats before sanding. Cure overnight before the sanding; longer, if the weather is humid.

9. Wrap a piece of #400 sandpaper over the padded side of a sanding block. Wet sandpaper with soap suds, and sand in a circular motion over all areas of the box. When the sides feel smooth, dry with a lint-free cloth or paper towel.

10. Brush on 4 additional coats of lacquer, and sand again. (The texture will still be rough and you will see the pearl flakes; I like it this way. If you prefer a fine smooth finish, brush on additional coats of lacquer until your pearl flakes are completely buried. Repeat the wet sandpaper polishing until your finish feels smooth.)

11. With #0000 steel wool, gently polish the sections of the box in a straight up and down motion to eliminate sandpaper scratches. Wipe with a lint-free cloth. Set aside to cure for 2 weeks.

12. Press down aluminum foil against the sides and bottoms of the box for a lining pattern. Cut foil. Cut cardboard according to the foil pattern. Trim ⅛ inch to ¼ inch from all edges of the cardboard to allow for fabric turn-under. (The amount you must trim to permit a snug lining fit will depend on the thickness of your lining fabric. You will have to check the measurements when your lining is cut and make the necessary adjustments.)

13. Cut lining according to your cardboard pieces, adding ½ inch for fabric turn-under on all edges.

14. *Optional:* Following cardboard pattern, cut a piece of foam shipping material or artfoam for padding for the bottom of the purse lining.

15. Thin white glue with water. Working on waxed paper, glue the ½-inch fabric turn-under allowance to the wrong side of the cardboard pieces on all edges. See *Diagram.* Check to see whether pieces fit before permitting glue to dry. If pieces are too tight, trim cardboard and reglue. Let all fabric-covered pieces dry overnight. Check fitting again; make final adjustments. Glue the finished pieces into the box; glue the side pieces first, the foam padding on the bottom next, and the bottom piece last. (Save a piece of lining material; you can lift out a soiled section of this lining and replace the section without disturbing the entire lining.)

16. Follow same lining procedure for lid of box.

17. Place the top and bottom of the box together; hold in position with rubber bands. Measure carefully to place hinges on the back edges, equally distant from the ends of the box. Mark placement for screw holes with a pencil; remove the hinges. Start holes for screws with an awl. Place the hinges again; set in screws about halfway and then go back and tighten screws. Remove rubber bands.

18. Measure carefully to place the catch midway between the ends of the front. Mark placement for screw holes; proceed as with the hinges.

19. Attach handle in the same manner, measuring equal distances from the ends of the lid for the placement of the handle hardware. If you use an old necklace as a handle, attach it to screw-in eye hooks.

20. Attach a decorative ball foot at each of the 4 corners of the box bottom to prevent scratching of finish.

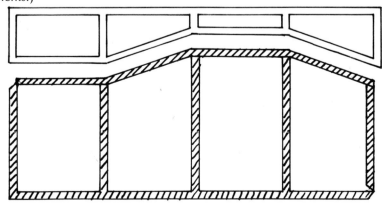

Repousséd Hand Mirror

It must be that superstitious streak in me that makes me reluctant to throw away an old hand mirror, even when it's damaged. When the back of my mirror became badly dented, I repaired the back with gesso, painted it pink, decorated it with prints of Boucher cherubs, and raised parts of the cherubs' bodies in repoussé. To my surprise I found I liked my repaired mirror better than the original.

Materials

old hand mirror
vinegar
gesso or wood putty (optional: for repair of cracks in mirror)
#220, #400, and #600 sandpaper
acrylic paint in color of your choice
decoupage sealer
2 identical prints or greeting cards
decoupage or manicure scissors
white glue
brayer
Decal-it or transfer medium of your choice

bread dough: 3 slices white bread, 3 tablespoons white glue, 3 drops lemon juice, 3 drops glycerine
spray finish
#0000 steel wool
decoupage wax
small piece of felt (could be from man's old hat)

Procedure

1. Wash mirror in a vinegar and water solution. Dry carefully.

2. Repair and fill in cracks with gesso or wood putty, depending on the extent of the damage. Sand well, starting with #220 sandpaper and ending with #600. Cover the mirror glass with paper and masking tape. Brush a coat of gesso over the back of the mirror. Let dry. Sand again.

3. Brush 2 coats of acrylic paint on back, handle, and frame of face, allowing drying time and sanding between coats. Let dry.

4. Seal one of your prints or greeting cards with 3 misty coats of decoupage sealer, allowing drying time between coats.

5. From the sealed print or greeting card, cut out the figure(s) you intend to put on the back of your mirror. Using decoupage or manicure scissors, hold curved point of the scissors pointed away from the print at a 45-degree angle. Hold your cutting hand still except to open and close the scissor blades; with your other hand, feed the print into the scissor blades.

6. Wet the back of the cutout print with water and then apply white glue; glue print to the back of the mirror. Roll out excess glue and air bubbles with a brayer over a slightly dampened paper towel. Roll from the center out to the edges. If air bubbles develop, prick the print with a straight pin and roll again. Wipe off any glue residue on the print. Let dry overnight.

7. Brush a coat of Decal-it over the second print or greeting card, brushing evenly across and then up and down in smooth strokes. Let dry for 15 minutes. Brush on 5 additional coats, brushing in alternate directions with each application and allowing 15 minutes drying time between each application. Cure print for 2 hours.

8. Soak the print overnight in warm water.

9. Meanwhile, prepare bread dough mixture. Remove crusts, tear bread into small pieces, and place in a bowl. Add glue, glycerine, and lemon juice. Mix together with fingers; knead until mixture has a smooth texture and does not stick to fingers. Store in plastic bag; refrigerate overnight.

10. Remove the print from the water, and lay it face down on a smooth surface near water. Peel paper from the back of the print; rub gently with a sponge or a washcloth to remove every trace of paper. Keep one hand flat on the print while rubbing with the other. Your print will now be like transparent film; be careful not to tear or stretch.

11. Apply Decal-it to the back of the film-like print. Let dry.

12. Cut out the portion from the film-like print you intend to raise for depth. (On the cherubs, I raised bows, stomachs, and buttocks.)

13. Remove bread dough from refrigerator. Apply white glue to the area on the first print that you'd like to elevate. Place a small mound of bread dough over that area, enough to achieve the depth you desire. Be sure enough glue remains at the edge of the mound to make the edges of the cutout adhere to the flat print. Stretch the film-like print portions over the top of the bread dough mound. Continue in this manner until all areas that you wish to elevate are raised. Let dry overnight.

14. Apply 10 coats of spray finish over the mirror (do not spray the glass), allowing about 30 minutes drying time between coats. Drying conditions will vary, so be sure that each coat is completely dry before applying any subsequent coat of finish. Test by touching with your knuckle when you think finish is dry; if your knuckle leaves an imprint, you need additional drying time. Let cure overnight before sanding.

15. Sand gently all painted sections on the mirror and the repoussé prints with a piece of #600 sandpaper over the padded side of a sanding block; wet sandpaper with soap suds, and sand in a circular motion. When the finish feels smooth, dry with a lint-free rag or paper towel.

16. Apply several additional coats of finish. Repeat the sanding procedure as directed.

17. With #0000 steel wool, gently polish the painted and decorated surface in a straight up and down motion to eliminate sandpaper scratches. The more you polish, the prettier the finish will become. Wipe with a lint-free cloth. Set aside for 2 weeks before you polish.

18. Apply a light coat of decoupage wax over the mirror (again, not the glass). Polish in a circular motion with a small piece of felt. Remove protective paper and masking tape from mirror glass.

Paint Bucket Curler Caddy

If you need a place to store hair curlers, don't throw away a patterned washcloth that has begun to show signs of wear or a gift washcloth that doesn't fit into your bathroom color scheme. By combining it with a paper paint bucket, you can provide yourself with a pretty and useful curler caddy.

Materials

paper paint bucket
gesso
acrylic paint in a color compatible with washcloth cutout
clear acrylic spray
washcloth with pattern that can be cut out (mine had butterflies)
Plasti-tak
Velverette Craft Glue
ball fringe in color of your choice to encircle top of bucket

Procedure

1. Apply a coat of gesso to the outside of the paint bucket for stability and body.

2. Brush on 2 coats of acrylic paint outside bucket, allowing drying time between coats.

3. Apply 2 misty coats of clear acrylic spray to outside, allowing drying time between coats.

4. Cut out designs from washcloth and plan composition on bucket; set in place with Plasti-tak.

5. Glue cutouts in place with Velverette Craft Glue, removing Plasti-tak as you glue.

6. Glue ball fringe around the top edges of the bucket, letting the straight edge of the fringe overlap the top inside edge of the bucket.

Immortalized Wedding Invitation

People frequently bring wedding invitations into the store and ask what they can do to preserve them, either as a family memento or as a special gift to the bride and groom. One of the most attractive ways is to decal them to a wedding greeting card and then decoupage them to a wooden plaque. You can use this same idea with a birth announcement or an invitation to a Bar Mitzvah or a silver or golden wedding anniversary party.

If possible, have the invitation unfolded and hand delivered. That way you'll eliminate wrinkles and folds and your work will be much easier.

Materials

wedding invitation
Decal-it
wood for plaque: size to suit card, preferably
    with decorative routed border
#220 and #400 sandpaper

decoupage sealer
white acrylic paint
Lustre Wax, Rub 'n Buff, Treasure Gold, or Liquid
    Leaf in antique gold color
turpentine (not necessary with Liquid Leaf)
wedding greeting card
white glue
brayer
Mona Lisa finish or lacquer finish of your choice
#0000 steel wool
gold decoupage braid for 4 edges of plaque
antiquing glaze of your choice
decoupage wax
waxed paper
small piece of felt (could be from man's old hat)
wedding gift wrapping paper (for back of
    plaque)
zip-off ring from soda can or saw-toothed metal
    picture hanger

Procedure

1. Brush 8 coats of Decal-it over the invitation, allowing 30 minutes drying time between coats. Brush coats in alternate directions with each application. Allow the final coat to cure overnight.
2. Sand plaque, starting with #220 sandpaper and ending with #400. Seal both sides of the wood with decoupage sealer. Let dry.
3. Brush white acrylic paint over both sides of the wood. Let dry.
4. Dilute a small amount of Lustre Wax, Rub 'n Buff, or Treasure Gold with turpentine on a small piece of aluminum foil. (You may use Liquid Leaf, but do not dilute it with turpentine.) Brush on gold over the routed decorative edges of the wood. Let set. Wipe off excess with a textured paper towel. Let dry.
5. If you are using a shaped board or if the greeting card is larger than your board, shape the card to the board by placing the card on the board and running your finger around the edges to make an imprint of the size and shape. Cut your card to fit the face of the board.
6. Sponge the back of the card with water. Glue the card to the board with white glue. Roll out excess glue and air bubbles with a brayer over a dampened paper towel. If air bubbles develop, prick with a pin and roll again. Let dry.

7. Soak the invitation overnight in warm water. Remove the print from the water, and lay face down on a smooth surface near water. Carefully rub the paper away from the back of the print. Be careful not to rub through the paper or to tear or stretch the print. When most of the paper has been removed, rub gently with a sponge or a washcloth to remove every last trace of paper.

8. When all of the paper has been removed, apply Decal-it to the back of the print. Let dry. Do not worry if the invitation looks cloudy; it will dry clear.

9. Plan the placement of your invitation on your wedding greeting card and trim the invitation to fit.

10. Brush Decal-it over the back of the invitation and on the area of the card where you plan to glue the invitation. Press in place. Roll out excess glue and air bubbles with a brayer over a dampened paper towel. Roll from the center to the outward edges. If air bubbles develop, prick with a pin and roll again. Let dry.

11. Brush Decal-it over the entire picture. Let dry overnight.

12. When thoroughly dry, brush on your first coat of lacquer, following directions for application on the label. Note drying time: Be aware that the greatest problem in decoupage is the cracking of finish, which occurs when moisture has been sealed in because of inadequate drying time. Apply at least 10 coats of finish before sanding. Cure overnight before the first sanding; longer if the weather is humid.

13. Wrap sandpaper over the padded side of your sanding block. Wet sandpaper with soap suds and sand in a circular motion. When the plaque feels smooth, dry well with a lint-free cloth or a paper towel.

14. Continue to apply subsequent coats of lacquer, allowing adequate drying time between coats, until you can no longer feel the edge of the invitation. Wet the sandpaper again and repeat the sanding procedure as directed. Dry with a lint-free cloth or paper towel.

15. With #0000 steel wool, gently polish the plaque in a straight up and down motion to eliminate the sandpaper scratches. The more you polish, the prettier the finish will become. Wipe with a lint-free cloth.

16. Seal braid with 3 misty coats of decoupage sealer, allowing drying time after each coat.

17. Apply antiquing glaze using directions on the label. Pat away excess glaze with facial tissue. Let dry.

18. Seal antiquing with 3 misty coats of decoupage sealer, allowing drying time between coats. Let dry completely.

19. Cut the braid into 4 pieces, each slightly longer than the sides of the plaque. Place the braid face down on waxed paper and lightly brush on white glue to the back of the braid; allow to set until it becomes sticky. Glue the braid around the edges of the card, overlapping braid at the corners. Mitre corners by cutting diagonally through the overlapped braid. Press the braid down with the wide edge of the burnisher. Wipe off excess glue. Let dry.

20. Carefully brush on 2 coats of lacquer over the braid to protect it. Try not to spread the finish over the rest of the plaque. Set aside to cure for 2 weeks before waxing.

21. Apply a light coat of decoupage wax over the face of the plaque. Polish in a circular motion with a small piece of felt.

22. Cut out gift wrapping paper to fit the back of the plaque. Glue to the back with white glue. Roll out excess glue and air bubbles with a brayer.

23. Center and attach a zip-off ring from a soda can or a saw-toothed metal hanger to the back of the plaque near the top.

VARIATION: Preserve a birth announcement in the same way with suitable card and wrapping paper.

Man's Personalized Wastepaper Basket

(See completed project on page 19.)

If you've ever been at a loss for a way to honor a man's business promotion or award, here is an answer: Give him a personalized wastepaper basket for his office or den. Use the article and the picture describing his promotion or award as it appeared in the local newspaper, as well as the paper's masthead.

If you are working to raise funds, this wastepaper basket with the *Wall Street Journal* or the stock market page is a good choice, even if it is not personalized. Because such a variety of companies are listed on the financial pages, chances are good that a buyer will find the company of his choice.

Materials

page of a newspaper
instant decoupage (Fun Podge, Mod Podge, Decollage)
metal wastepaper basket with inside painted black, red, or gold (choose a round or oval basket with straight vertical sides, not one that slants inward toward the bottom)
brayer
newspaper article about personal achievement, preferably with picture
black Mystik Tape, ¾-inch roll
masthead of local newspaper
shirt cardboard
white glue (optional)
acrylic spray

Procedure

1. Cut pages from a newspaper to fit around wastepaper basket, keeping top and bottom edges flush.
2. Brush instant decoupage over the exterior of the basket. Let dry.
3. Starting at a side seam of the basket, apply a coat of instant decoupage to one-quarter of the wastebasket and to the back of the newspaper that will cover the area. Glue newspaper in place. Roll out excess glue and air bubbles with a brayer over a dampened paper towel. Roll from the center out to the corners. If an air bubble develops, prick with a pin and roll again. Continue in the same manner until the entire wastepaper basket is covered. Let dry.
4. Center a newspaper write-up (about a personal achievement) to one side of the basket and glue with instant decoupage. Roll with a brayer over a dampened paper towel.
5. Apply another coat of instant decoupage over the outside of the basket. Let dry.
6. Cut 2 pieces of black Mystik Tape to cover basket side seams; press in place. Apply black tape under the metal rim around the top and bottom edges of the basket; butt ends.
7. Cut out newspaper masthead, cutting away excess paper. Cut a piece of cardboard the same size as the newspaper masthead to elevate the title. Glue together with instant decoupage, brushing a coat on the cardboard and on the back of the masthead. Let dry. (If you wish, you may glue the masthead flat without elevating it on cardboard. Use instant decoupage to glue it, if you choose this method.)
8. Center and glue cardboard with white glue to the side of the basket opposite the article, directly below the top Mystik Tape edging. Place a weight on it, and let dry.
9. Spray wastepaper basket with several misty coats of acrylic spray, allowing drying time between coats.

Child's Drawing Plaque

(See completed project on page 83.)

I'm one of those grandmothers who brag and carry photographs and display everything made by their grandchildren. Among my most treasured possessions are some of my granddaughter Cary's crayon drawings preserved on plaques.

Materials

wood: size to suit drawing, preferably with decorative routed border
#220 sandpaper
gesso
white acrylic paint
acrylic paint in color of your choice (optional: for routed border)
instant decoupage (Fun Podge, Mod Podge, Decollage)
child's crayon drawing
brayer
zip-off ring from soda can or saw-toothed metal picture hanger

Procedure

1. Sand wood well. Brush on a coat of gesso over all sides. Let dry.

2. Apply 2 coats of white acrylic paint over all sides, allowing drying time between coats. Let dry.

3. *Optional:* Paint the routed edge of the wood in one of the colors in the drawing. When dry, apply a second coat, and let dry.

4. Brush instant decoupage over all sides of the wood. Allow to dry.

5. Brush another coat of instant decoupage on the face of the wood. Brush instant decoupage on the back of a child's crayon drawing; position on the wood and press down. Roll out excess glue and air bubbles with a brayer over a dampened paper towel. Roll from the center out to each of the 4 corners. Let dry.

6. Brush 2 additional coats of instant decoupage over the face of the plaque, allowing drying time between coats.

7. Attach a zip-off ring from a soda can or a saw-toothed metal hanger to the back of the plaque.

VARIATION: Stain the wood instead of painting it. Omit gesso.

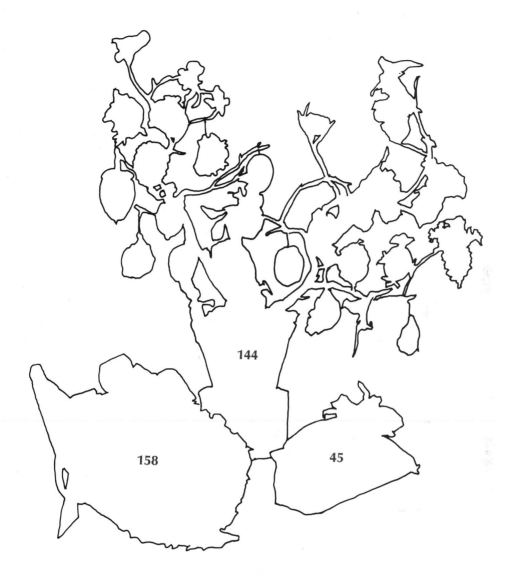

144

158

45

Details and instructions for projects shown may be found on page number indicated

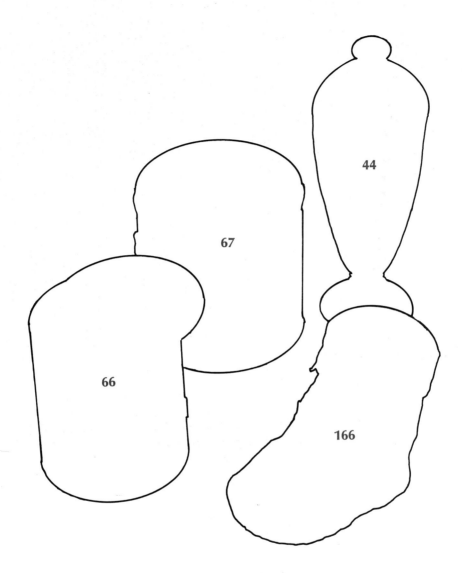

Details and instructions for projects shown may be found on page number indicated

Chapter
4

Projects for Beginners

Postage Stamp Collage
Tin Can Pincushion
Ladybug Stringholder
Chunk Candle
Decotiqued Key Ring
Egg Carton Flower
"Nutty" Centerpiece
Peach and Olive Pit Plaque
Seashell Mobile
Felt Caterpillar
Coat Hanger Sculpture
Six-pack Picture Frames
China Repair
Driftwood Name Pin
Block and Spool Mirror
Snake Pull-Toy
Electrical Cord Holder
Crystallized Pin Tray

This chapter presents projects for beginners who are untrained in craft techniques and for persons of all ages who would like to create something lovely but lack either the dexterity or the time and patience for more complex crafts. The careful craftsmanship called for in other chapters still applies, but these easier projects require fewer materials and call for less time between steps.

Futhermore, the projects are relatively inexpensive, which makes them ideal for groups such as Scout troops, hospitalized or handicapped persons, Sunday schools, and people in rest homes. The leaders of these groups usually must operate with extremely limited funds. I always suggest that they ask friends and relatives to donate supplies: leftover fabric, felt, trims, buttons, wood, paper, used containers—in fact, the same throwaway items this book discusses.

1518
U.S. Savanah

Postage Stamp Collage

(See completed project on page 83.)

Don't throw away used postage stamps. Take a picture of your choice and cover it with postage stamps glued at random angles to form an attractive collage.

Materials

used postage stamps
white glue
picture of your choice (I chose a picture of a ship with a solid background)
cardboard backing for picture
spray finish
frame of your choice to fit picture

Procedure

1. Remove postage stamps from envelopes; soak in water if difficult to remove. Separate stamps into piles according to color.
2. Glue your picture to cardboard backing.
3. Glue the stamps over details in your picture. (I followed the general rules of color arrangement, using darker shades of stamps at the base of my picture for the ship bottom and lighter ones at the top for the sails. But there are no real rules for stamp placement. If you think you have a good idea for color arrangement in your picture, break all the rules.) Place stamps at odd angles and overlap edges. Let glue dry thoroughly.
4. When dry, apply 2 misty coats of spray finish to the picture, allowing drying time between coats.
5. Frame picture in the frame of your choice.

114

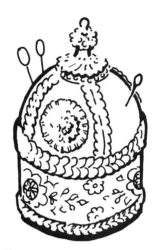

Tin Can Pincushion

(See completed project on page 16.)

Here's an easy way to use several leftovers creatively. Collect your leftover trims from making Christmas ornaments or decorating Easter eggs: embroidered braid or decorative ribbon braid, metallic braid, guimpe braid, a costume jewel, a single earring, or a corsage pin and bead. With these and an empty tuna fish can, you can make the prettiest pincushion you ever saw.

Materials

tuna fish can
vinegar
small bag patching cement or plaster of Paris
Styrofoam ball to fit snugly inside tuna fish can
felt in colors of your choice (I used purple for
    the top of the pincushion and green for the
    base)
Velverette Craft Glue
embroidered braid or ribbon braid to encircle
    and cover side of can (I used a floral
    pattern)
guimpe braid to encircle can twice (I used
    lavender)
narrow gold metallic braid to go across top of
    pincushion twice
single earring, jewel, or bead and corsage pin

Procedure

1. Wash tuna fish can in a vinegar and water solution. Dry well.
2. Mix a small amount of patching cement or plaster of Paris, according to directions on the package, and fill three-quarters of the can. When it is almost set, insert the Styrofoam ball into the plaster. Let dry.
3. Cut a felt circle large enough to cover the exposed part of the Styrofoam plus ¼-inch overhang on top of can. Spread Velverette Craft Glue over one side of the felt. Stretch the glued side over the Styrofoam; hold felt in place with T-straight pins all around the edges. Remove pins when glue is dry.
4. Glue embroidered braid around the sides of the can, covering the felt overhang on the top edge. If braid is not wide enough to cover the sides and overlap the edges of the felt, center and glue the braid on the side. Butt ends of braid; dip cut ends of braid in glue to prevent raveling.
5. Cut a piece of felt to fit the bottom of the can; glue in place with Velverette Craft Glue.
6. Divide the felt-covered top of the Styrofoam ball into 2 sections by gluing gold metallic braid across the center of the ball from one edge of the can to the opposite side. Now divide the ball into 4 equal sections by gluing braid in the opposite direction, forming right angles and crossing the first braid glued at the center.
7. Glue guimpe braid around the top and bottom side edges of the can, overlapping the edges of the embroidered braid already glued.
8. Glue a costume jewel or single earring to the center top of the pincushion, or insert a corsage pin into a bead, and insert into the center top of the pincushion.

VARIATION: Decorate a matching what-not box for a bureau in the same manner or perhaps a shoe box such as the one described below. (See completed projects on page 16.)

Materials

plastic-coated shoe box with lid
felt to cover outside of lid and inside and outside of box
Velverette Craft Glue
embroidered braid to go around sides of box
guimpe braid to go around sides of box twice and lid once
4 decorative ball feet
narrow metallic braid to encircle lid once
9 costume jewels

Procedure

1. Cut felt to fit the inside sides of the shoe box, allowing an extra ½ inch on the bottom edges and an extra 1 inch on the top edges. Cut felt in a continuous piece if you have enough fabric; cut in pieces if you do not. Apply Velverette Craft Glue to one side of the felt. Glue sides in place on the inside of the box, gluing the ½-inch allowance to the inside bottom and turning the top 1-inch allowance over the inside top edges and gluing in place to the outside sides.

2. Cut felt to fit the inside bottom of the box, covering the ½-inch overlap from the sides. Check fit; glue in place.

3. Cut felt to fit the outside bottom of the box, allowing an extra 1 inch on all sides. Glue in place, allowing the 1-inch felt turnover to come up to the box's outside sides.

4. Glue embroidered braid around the sides of the box, covering the felt turnover on the top and bottom edges. If braid is not wide enough to overlap the felt, glue a strip of felt wide enough to cover the exposed areas and overlap the edges of the felt; then center and glue the braid on this strip. Butt ends of braid; dip cut ends of braid in glue to prevent raveling.

5. Glue guimpe braid around the top and bottom edges of the box.

6. Glue decorative feet to the 4 bottom corners of the box.

7. Cut felt to fit exactly the outside lid of the box; glue to lid. Glue narrow metallic braid around the 4 sides of the lid, leaving room at bottom for lid to fit inside box. Glue guimpe braid around the 4 top edges of the lid.

8. Glue a decorative jewel to the center top of the lid, one to each side of it, one to each corner, and one to the center of each long side.

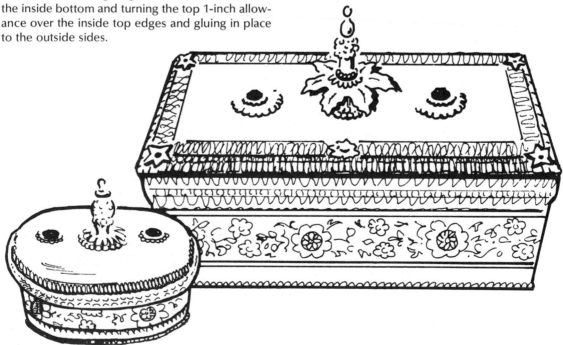

Ladybug Stringholder

(See completed project on page 4.)

Don't throw away a small piece of leftover burlap or scraps of felt. Make a useful bag to keep your string from tangling as you wrap packages or tie back the legs of a turkey. Hang it on the back of a door or on a hook in the kitchen. To decorate it, you can trace any pattern that appeals to you from a coloring book, a greeting card, a wallpaper design. Then, cut out the design from felt and glue it to the front of the bag.

Materials

small piece of burlap: 20 × 10 inches
scraps of felt: colors to suit designs
tracing paper
eyelet and eyelet punch
white glue
2 metal rings
ball of string

Procedure

1. Fold burlap fabric in half lengthwise, *wrong* sides together. Press a crease into the bottom fold line with your finger. (The piece should now be 2 folds of fabric, each 10 inches × 10 inches.) Open the piece out to the original 20- × 10-inch measurement, and work with the upper half as the bag front.

2. In the center bag front, 8½ inches from the top, use an eyelet punch to make an eyelet opening for string to come through (or, with scissors, make a small hole about ½ inch in diameter, and finish the edges with a buttonhole stitch).

3. Trace and enlarge design from the diagram or a coloring book or wallpaper pattern. Cut out pieces of the design from scraps of felt. Plan placement on the burlap; do not go beyond a 1-inch margin on either side of the front of the burlap bag (upper half of the burlap), and do not go below the crease made with your finger. Glue pieces of felt in place and let dry. (If you are using our pattern, cut out ladybug body, head, and feelers from black felt and glue in place. Cut out wings from red felt and glue in place over body. Cut body spots from black felt and glue in place over wings.)

4. Fold burlap in half lengthwise, right sides together. Stitch both sides of the bag in a ¾-inch seam. Turn to the right side. Press seams.

5. Turn under a ¾-inch top hem to the inside of the bag. Stitch flat.

6. Sew a metal ring to the back of the upper right corner of the bag for hanging. Sew another metal ring to the bottom front of the bag, on the fold line, 1 inch in from the right bottom corner; see diagram.

7. Put a ball of string into the bag. Pull the end through the center eyelet hole. Pass it through the bottom metal ring and let the string hang.

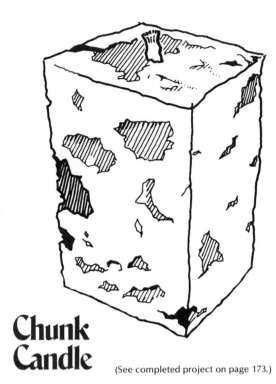

Chunk Candle

(See completed project on page 173.)

It's fascinating and fun to watch an old craft experience a renaissance in popularity and to see the craft techniques associated with that craft improve. Such a craft is candlemaking—an old art that is extremely popular today.

Candles have never been easier or more economical to make, and they have never been prettier. Here are the directions for a candle that is as handsome as any you'll find in a store; it is made out of those stubby ends of used candles that you ordinarily throw away.

Materials

small pieces of used candles in various colors
slab candle wax (low-temperature wax, usually sold in 11-pound blocks; one block will make four 1-quart-sized candles)
double boiler, or melting pot and pan of water (an old coffee pot or pitcher is good for heating and pouring wax)
candy thermometer
stearic acid or hardening crystals (optional)
wooden spoon or dowel
cardboard milk carton in size of your choice
aluminum pie plate or cookie sheet

1 ready-made candle (a wobbly, broken, or an odd candle that is as tall as you wish to make your chunk candle)
wire candle wick (optional: if you do not have an old candle to use in the center)
old nylon stocking or panty hose

Procedure

1. Cut or break bits of used candles into small, irregular-shaped chunks. Set aside.
2. With a hammer or ice pick, break the slab of candle wax ito pieces small enough to go into the top of a double boiler or into a melting pot set in a pan of water. Heat wax to a temperature of 145 degrees; check temperature with a candy thermometer. Be careful not to get water into the wax. *Do not leave hot wax unattended;* remove from the heat if you must leave it even for a moment.
3. *Optional:* Add to the hot wax 3 tablespoons of stearic acid or hardening crystals per pound of wax. Stir with a wooden spoon or dowel.
4. Make sure your milk carton mold is clean and dry. Place mold in aluminum pie plate or cookie sheet with newspaper underneath mold.
5. Cut the ready-made candle at the bottom to fit the size of the candle you plan to make if it is not already the correct size. Insert the candle into the center of the milk carton, and secure by pouring into the bottom a ½-inch layer of hot wax; let harden. (This will enable the wax you pour later to build up around the side of the candle, and you will not have to insert a wick. If you do not have a candle, you can insert a wick when your candle is made.)
6. Drop some used candle pieces into the bottom of the mold to make a layer 3 inches deep. Pour melted slab wax (temperature 145 degrees; reheat if necessary) to within ½ inch of the top of used candle bits. Add 3 inches more of used candle bits; pour melted wax to within ½ inch of this layer. Continue until you reach the desired candle height. End with a layer of melted slab wax.
7. If your candle develops a well in the center, heat some more wax and use to fill this well about 1 hour after pouring the candle. Save leftover wax in a separate container to use again; don't let it harden in the melting pot.
8. Cool candle at room temperature, *not* in the refrigerator. When cool, tear away the milk carton and remove candle.

9. *Optional:* If you did not use an old candle as the center, insert a wick now. Heat an ice pick; use it to make a hole in the center of the candle. Insert the wick into the candle hole. Fill the hole with hot melted wax.

10. Polish the seam lines of the candle and remove blemishes by rubbing candle with an old nylon stocking or panty hose.

Decotiqued Key Ring

There's a craft called Decotiquing that's done much like children's Rub-ons. A Decotique is a dry transfer that can be rubbed onto any clean, hard surface with a wooden tongue depressor, a popsicle stick, or the flat of your fingernail. It can be used to apply a hand-painted look to pocketbooks, boxes, trays, and furniture. Small scraps of plywood cut into squares, circles, and diamond shapes and drilled to make a hole can be decorated to make key chains that look hand-painted.

Materials

scraps of ⅛-inch plywood, cut to desired shape (I used a diamond-shaped piece, 2½ inches long on each side)
#220 sandpaper
gesso or decoupage sealer
acrylic paint in color of your choice
Decotique pattern of your choice
spray finish
antiquing glaze of your choice (optional)
key chain

Procedure

1. Drill a hole in the wood about ¼ inch from an edge for the key chain. Sand the edges well.

2. If wood is not in good condition, brush a coat of gesso on both sides; let dry. If wood is in good condition, brush or spray a coat of decoupage sealer over both sides.

3. Brush on 2 coats of acrylic paint, allowing drying time between coats.

4. Cut out from the full sheet of patterns the Decotique pattern you intend to use. Check to see that it fits on your wood. Measure to center and position correctly.

5. Place design on the wood with the white tacky side down. With the wooden applicator, rub the design from the center out to each of the 4 corners (it's better to rub too gently than too hard). Peel surface paper gently away from the corners to see whether pattern has adhered properly. If you've missed an area, return paper to its former position and rub again.

6. Peel off paper. If the pattern is not firmly attached, rub gently with your fingers until it adheres tightly.

7. Apply spray finish over the front and back of the wood; allow to dry.

8. *Optional:* Apply a coat of antiquing glaze to the front and back of the wood, according to directions on the label. Wipe off excess with a textured paper towel. Let dry overnight.

9. Apply 2 misty coats of spray finish, allowing drying time between coats.

10. Insert key chain into drilled hole.

Egg Carton Flower

If you're fortunate enough to be able to purchase your eggs in shiny, pearl-finish plastic egg cartons, don't throw the cartons away. These cartons are easy to cut with ordinary scissors and can be shaped into ever-so-many different objects. But perhaps because of the variety in color, they are most often used in floral arrangements.

This floral decoration is an especially easy and inexpensive project for a Scout group. Send out a call to troop parents for contributions of plastic egg cartons, buttons, the leaves and calyxes from old plastic flowers, and flat-topped detergent bottle caps or small spray-can tops.

Materials

plastic egg carton in color of your choice
#19 wire
button, ¾ inch wide (preferably a shank button with a flat bottom)
leaf and calyx from old plastic flower
Stickum
green florist tape
top from detergent bottle or small spray can
acrylic paint in color compatible with color scheme (optional)
plaster of Paris or Sculptamold
small-size colored gravel for pools or fish tanks

Procedure

1. With scissors, cut out an egg cup from the plastic carton. Cut away plastic around the edges of the cup so that 1 inch remains above the curve in the egg cup bottom.

2. Cut 8 petals by making 4 equally distant cuts into the egg cup as far as the bottom curve and then dividing each of the 4 petals into 2 petals.

3. Cut each petal in a rounded shape, or cut to a point in the center top of each petal.

4. With the sharp pointed tip of the scissors, make 2 holes for wire in the bottom of the egg cup.

5. Cut a 6-inch length of wire. From the outside, insert one end of the wire up through one of the holes in the egg cup bottom. Put the wire through the shank of the button, bend it, and bring it down through the second hole in the egg cup bottom to meet the other end of the wire; twist the wire ends together. (If you are using a button with holes, bring the wire up through one hole in the button, bend it, bring it down through another hole in the button, through the second hole in the egg cup, and out to meet the other end of the wire.)

6. Remove the calyx from an old plastic flower (or purchase a package of calyxes at a craft store if you are doing a quantity of flowers). Attach a dab of Stickum to the bottom of the egg cup flower, push the calyx up the ends of wire, and adhere it to the bottom of the flower.

7. Wrap wire with green florist tape; tape a plastic leaf into the wire midway as you wind the green tape.

8. If you are not satisfied with the color of the detergent cap or spray-can top, paint it with an acrylic color compatible with your color scheme. Let dry.

9. Mix a small quantity of plaster of Paris or Sculptamold, according to directions on the package. Fill cap with mixture; let set slightly. Cover the top of the cement with gravel.

10. When almost dry, insert wired flower into cap and let harden.

"Nutty" Centerpiece

(See completed project on page 3.)

Don't throw away a chocolate frozen pudding container or old nylon stockings or panty hose. Use them with nuts and a Styrofoam cone to make an interesting autumn table centerpiece.

Nuts once had to be wired before they could be put into an arrangement, and that was quite a chore. Then I discovered that if you cut old nylon stockings into small squares and wire the fabric around the nuts, you can make quick and easy wired nuts that can be used in many kinds of flower and fruit arrangements. The sheer hosiery cannot be seen when pulled tightly around the nuts.

Materials

brown plastic frozen pudding container (small or large, depending on size of arrangement you want)
Stickum
Styrofoam to fit inside container
Styrofoam cone: 12 inches high for large container, 9 inches high for small container
#23 wire
a pair of old nylon stockings or panty hose in light shade
mixed nuts in their shells
instant spray finish (optional)
artificial squirrel

Procedure

1. Attach a piece of Stickum to the inside bottom of the pudding container. Cut a piece of Styrofoam to fit inside the container and set in place over the Stickum.
2. Insert several toothpicks into the top of the Styrofoam, allowing one end of each toothpick to extend 1 inch over the top of the Styrofoam.
3. Insert the base of the Styrofoam cone into the protruding toothpicks.
4. Cut wire into 6-inch pieces. Cut hosiery into 4-inch squares. Wrap a hosiery square tightly around each nut and secure with a piece of wire; see the diagram. Cut away excess hosiery fabric and press the 2 lengths of wire closely together. Continue covering and wiring nuts until you have enough to cover the entire outside of the cone.
5. Insert wired nuts into the cone, starting at the bottom and working toward the top; fill in all areas.
6. *Optional:* For a shiny look, spray arrangement with 2 misty coats of instant finish, allowing drying time between coats.
7. Wrap a piece of wire around an artificial squirrel. Insert the ends of the wire into the Styrofoam at the edge of the container.

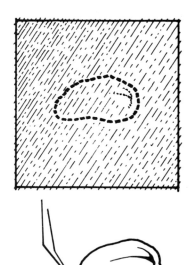

Peach and Olive Pit Plaque

(See completed project on page 83.)

When my children were still fussy eaters I often admonished them with the motto: Waste not, want not. As it is also a good motto for a don't-throw-it-away advocate, I recently designed a plaque for my office that features the motto. The whole project is made out of the most natural materials: peach and olive pits, split peas, and sawdust! You might use this idea to preserve your family's favorite motto.

Materials

peach and olive pits and split peas (the number is determined by the size of your plaque and length of your motto)
moss green acrylic spray paint
Dow Corning Urethane Bond Glue
canvas board or heavy cardboard in size of your choice, large enough to permit space for motto
sawdust (lumberyards will generally give you a bag of sawdust or wood shavings)
woodtone spray or brown acrylic spray paint
spray finish
zip-off ring from soda can or saw-toothed metal picture hanger

Procedure

1. Wash peach and olive pits well. Boil, if necessary, to get perfectly clean.
2. Spray olive pits with 2 misty coats of green spray paint. Let dry.
3. Spread glue over the face of the canvas board. Spread sawdust over the glue. Before the glue is completely dry, spray the sawdust with woodtone or brown paint.
4. Plan placement of motto on scrap paper first. Then, while sawdust is still pliable, use your fingers to trace the lettering of your motto.
5. Before the sawdust and glue base dries, begin to imbed the outside border with peach pits. Next, imbed inside border with olive pits. Fill in the motto lettering with split peas. Let dry completely.
6. Spray entire plaque with instant spray finish; let dry.
7. Attach a zip-off ring from a soda can or a saw-toothed metal picture hanger to the center back of the plaque near the top.

Procedure

1. With a knife, scratch a circular notch at 7 evenly spaced sections on the twig.

2. Cut fishing line in 5 pieces: two 9-inch pieces and three 11-inch pieces. Skipping notches on twig at either end, tie and knot the fishing line around the notches, alternating with a longer and a shorter piece of fishing line, starting and ending with the longer pieces. You will have 5 rows of line hanging down.

3. Make a hole in each shell with an awl or ice pick. Insert the line through the hole in the shell, and when the shell is placed in its proper location, knot it to the line. Knot the first shell on the longer pieces of line 1½ inches down from the twig; on the shorter pieces of line, knot the first shell 1 inch down from the twig. Knot each additional shell in each row 1 inch away from the last shell knotted. You will have 4 shells in each of the 5 rows.

4. Tie one end of the jute string around the end notch in the twig and knot securely; tie the other end of the string to the notch at the other end of the twig and knot. Your mobile is now ready to hang.

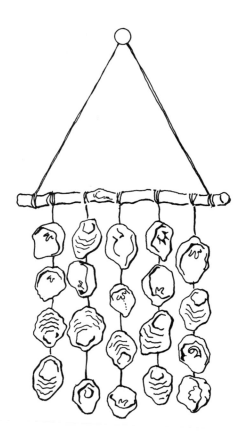

Seashell Mobile (See completed project on page 173.)

This project is for beachcombers and string savers. If you don't throw away short pieces of heavy string or the beautiful mementos of a beach vacation, you can make a seashell mobile. Hang it in a window or on a porch, and its music will remind you of the sea.

Materials

straight wooden twig, about 11 inches long and ¾ inch in diameter
fishing line, 1½ yards
seashells: 20 small, thin, pretty ones plus extras in case some break when making holes in them
awl or ice pick
heavy jute string, about ½ yard

124

Procedure

1. Use a compass to draw circles on cardboard in the following diameters: 1 inch, 1¼ inches, 1½ inches, 1¾ inches, 2 inches, 2¼ inches, 2½ inches, 2¾ inches, 3 inches, 3½ inches, 4 inches. Cut out circle patterns and use to cut out felt circles; cut each size circle from both main colors of felt.

2. See diagram to get facial feature patterns. For eyes, cut from felt scraps 2 gold circles, 2 white triangles, and 2 black pupils. From red felt, cut nose and mouth. Sew or glue parts of face to one of the two largest circles—the one in the color you want to "face forward."

3. On all circles that will "face backward" (except the smallest), center and sew the socket side of the snap. On all "forward" circles except the largest, center and sew the ball side of the snap. Sew snaps *firmly*.

4. Match contrasting colored circles according to size and so that one color faces forward and the other is on the back. Place each set of circles together with the snaps to the outside. Sew the edges of each set of circles in an overcast stitch, leaving an opening measuring about three-quarters of the way around. Fill each circle with nylon stockings for a plump look; then finish sewing the circle.

5. Snap the finished circles together.

6. Bend a pipe cleaner to resemble antennae. Sew in place in the center of the head between the eyes.

Felt Caterpillar (See completed project on page 7.)

Save old nylon stockings and panty hose to make this felt caterpillar for a child. More than a plaything, the caterpillar teaches children how to snap and unsnap their clothing. You can make this fellow as long as you want (I know a girl who made one 6 feet long!) and in any color combination that suits your fancy. Be forewarned that there's a fair amount of hand sewing in this project.

Materials

compass
several pieces of shirt cardboard
2 pieces of felt in contrasting colors, each
    approximately ¼ yard
small scraps of felt in black, red, white, and gold
10 large-sized snaps
old nylon stockings or panty hose
1 black pipe cleaner

Materials

wire coat hangers: heavy enough to hold shape,
  but not so heavy that wire can't be molded
wire cutters
fine wire or spool wire
pipe cleaners or colored wire
wooden block for base in suitable size
#220 sandpaper
awl or ice pick
acrylic spray paint in color or colors of your
  choice (optional)

Procedure

1. Cut off top of hanger with wire cutters; unbend hanger into a straight wire.
2. Start "sculpting" wherever you wish. Shape the wire as the figure in the diagram is shaped. When you have used all the wire in one hanger, overlap another hanger with the first one and wire the overlapped area together with fine wire or spool wire.
3. Use pipe cleaners or colored wire to shape eyes, ears, face, and hat. Join the pipe cleaners or wire to the wire hanger; turn in the edges.
4. Sand the edges of the wooden block base.
5. With an awl or ice pick, make a hole in the wooden base that extends from the top through to the bottom. With a U-shaped piece of wire turned upside down, fasten one of the man's feet to the top of the wooden base. Then bring the ends of the wire through the bottom of the base, twist together, bend so that they will lie perfectly flat, and tape down so that base will not wobble.
6. *Optional:* Spray wooden base and sculpture in color or colors of your choice.

Coat Hanger Sculpture

(See completed project on page 7.)

Most of us collect far more wire coat hangers than we can use, and end up throwing them away. Don't! Wire coat hangers can be bent and shaped into interesting and fun sculpture, such as the man in the project here. Children are especially inventive with wire sculpture, though adult supervision is recommended.

Six-pack Picture Frames

Don't throw away the plastic carrying handles that come on six packs of soda pop and beer. They make beautiful frames for snapshots and school pictures that you wish to display as a group.

Materials

heavy cardboard: amount will depend on number of pictures you wish to display (my cardboard measured 9 inches × 12 inches, for a grouping of 8 pictures)

black velveteen: a little more of this than the cardboard

white glue

black felt, same size as cardboard

plastic carrying handles from soda pop or beer packs: number will depend on number of pictures

gesso

Liquid Leaf, Rub 'n Buff, Lustre Wax, or Treasure Gold

turpentine (not necessary with Liquid Leaf)

Treasure Sealer

snapshots or school pictures

Quik Glue (an especially good glue for adhering plastic)

metallic gold braid to encircle edges of picture frames

zip-off ring from soda can or saw-toothed metal picture hanger

Procedure

1. Place velveteen fabric face down on a clean surface. Place cardboard on the fabric. Cut out fabric 1 inch larger than the cardboard on all sides. Cut away a small diagonal strip from each corner of the fabric to eliminate bulk.

2. Apply glue to the outside 1-inch border of the cardboard. Fold the edges of the material around the glued area, keeping corners tight and neat. (The diagonally cut corners of the fabric should give you a mitered corner edge when glued.)

3. Cut a piece of black felt to same size as the cardboard; then cut away ¼ inch on all edges of the felt. Glue felt to the back of the cardboard, covering the raw edges of the velvet.

4. Cut as many plastic circular frames from plastic carrying handles as you need for the number of pictures you have to frame. Place frame around each of your pictures and, with a pencil, trace outline. Cut out circular photos.

5. Brush a coat of gesso over the raised side of the plastic. Let dry.

6. Brush on a coat of Liquid Leaf, or dilute a small amount of Rub 'n Buff, Lustre Wax, or Treasure Gold with turpentine on a small piece of aluminum foil, and brush over the gesso-coated plastic. Let dry.

7. Apply a coat of Treasure Sealer over the gold and let dry.

8. With Quik Glue, glue plastic frames over the pictures, with gold side up.

9. Glue metallic braid around the edges of the plastic frames.

10. Plan placement of the frames on the velveteen-covered board; measure to ensure even margins. Glue the framed pictures in place. (Be careful not to get glue on the velvet; it is impossible to get off without leaving a mark.)

11. Attach a zip-off ring from a soda can or a saw-toothed metal picture hanger to the back of the cardboard in the center back near the top.

China Repair

A broken piece of your favorite china needn't leave you broken-hearted. You can repair a cracked plate or a chipped cup so well that you'll have trouble finding the damaged area.

In addition to being able to rescue your own china, you'll be able to salvage treasures from antique shops, where you can frequently purchase pieces of beautiful damaged china inexpensively.

Materials

**broken, chipped, or poorly mended piece of
    china (not glass)**
dishwasher detergent (optional)
tongs (optional)
dishcloth (optional)
fine-point artist's brush
Elmer's Glue
damp cloth
**sandbox, or shoe box filled with sand, Farina, or
    Ralston cereal**
masking tape
plastic margarine container or paper cup
white "dental stone" (available from dentist)
craft stick
#220 sandpaper
water colors and paintbrush (optional)
crystal clear epoxy glue (optional)
glaze (optional)

Procedure

1. Clean and dry piece to be repaired.
2. *Optional:* If piece was poorly mended, place it in pot with enough water to cover; add a handful of dishwasher detergent; let it come to a boil, and then lower heat and simmer for 10 minutes. If it does not boil apart, remove from pot with tongs, hold with a dishcloth, and apply slight pressure to break it apart.
3. Use fine-point paintbrush to "paint" on line of white glue over the broken "thickness" edge of only *one* of the pieces to be joined together. Begin and end your glued line ⅛ inch in from each edge. *Optional:* If china will be washed in a dishwasher, substitute epoxy glue and its commercial solvent for white glue; follow product directions.
4. Press broken pieces together until they fit as perfectly as possible. Rub your fingernail over the surface; if your nail catches on the broken area, try for a better fit. When fit is tight, wipe off excess glue with damp cloth. Check again to be sure fit is tight.
5. To hold piece until repair is set and glue dry, put glued piece on its side in a sandbox; don't let sand touch repaired area. If you are repairing a large plate or platter, cover back of glued area on the bottom of the plate with masking tape before setting in sandbox; remove tape when dry. Let dry undisturbed overnight.
6. If repair involves several pieces, glue one piece at a time, starting with the largest piece. Let each repair dry thoroughly in the sandbox before adding another piece.
7. To fill in chips on a broken piece, back the chipped area with masking tape to support it. Use a craft stick to mix equal parts of glue and water in a plastic container or paper cup; slowly add white "dental stone" until mixture is fairly thick in consistency (it should hold on a craft stick held upside down; if it falls off, add more powder). Mixture will set up quickly, so work fast. Apply mixture to chipped area, allowing a little more than needed for the repair (excess will be sanded away when set). If holes and crevices remain, place a small amount on your finger and spread it smoothly over the surface. Let dry overnight; remove masking tape when dry. Sand thoroughly with #220 sandpaper until smooth. Close your eyes and rub sanded surface with finger; it should feel perfectly smooth when sufficiently sanded. Throw container and excess mixture away; never pour down sink.
8. If paint or design on repaired piece needs retouching, paint the repaired area with water colors. If you need more than one color to repair damage, let each color dry before using another color. Brush a small amount of clear epoxy glue over the painted area to seal paint color and then apply a glaze. Let dry 24 hours.

4. Put a dab of glue on small piece of aluminum foil. Lift letters, one by one, with tweezers and dip in glue; attach to wood. Let glue dry thoroughly; letters will lift if glue is not completely dry.

5. Glue the pin backing to the back of the wood. Let dry.

6. Spray both sides of the pin with 2 misty coats of acrylic spray finish, allowing adequate drying time between coats.

Driftwood Name Pin

My grandchildren and I picked up several small pieces of driftwood on the beach one day. We glued on our names with letters from alphabet soup noodles and made pins as a memento of a happy summer afternoon.

These pins make fine gifts, name tags, or favors for a party. They're attractive, inexpensive, and quick to assemble in quantity. You can use a flat twig or a small piece of scrap wood if you don't have driftwood. You can paint the letters, spray them gold, or leave them natural.

Materials

small piece of driftwood, flat twig, or scrap wood: approximately 2 to 3 inches long × ¾ inch wide

white glue

box of alphabet soup noodles

acrylic paint in color of your choice (optional)

pin backing

acrylic spray finish

Procedure

1. Be sure wood is clean and thoroughly dry. Brush on a coat of glue to seal wood. Let dry.

2. Select alphabet soup letters to spell name, and place on cardboard.

3. *Optional:* Paint letters with acrylic paint in color of your choice. Let dry.

Block and Spool Mirror

(See completed project on page 54.)

Don't throw away an old mirror glass if it's in good condition. You can frame it with children's alphabet blocks and wooden sewing spools, and have a most colorful mirror for a child's bedroom.

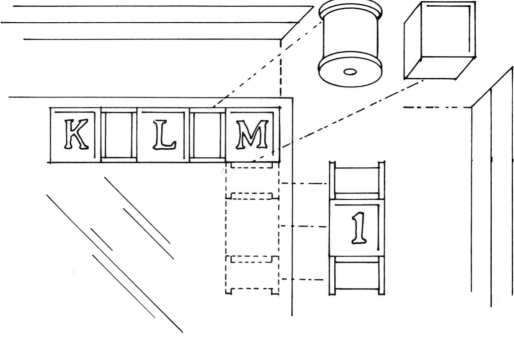

Materials

Masonite backing board

old mirror glass in size and shape of choice (my mirror was square, but it could be rectangular)

#220 sandpaper

mirror glue (available at a mirror or framing store)

children's alphabet building blocks, 1¼ inches on all sides (blocks and spools will be glued alternately around outside edges of mirror; number will be determined by size of mirror)

wooden sewing spools, 1¼ inches tall (wooden spools already painted are available by the bag in toy stores or save spools of equal size and paint your own)

acrylic spray paint in colors of your choice (optional: if spools need painting)

length of wire (for drying spools)

4 pieces of do-it-yourself framing to fit length and width of Masonite backing

acrylic paint for framing in color of your choice (optional)

spray finish (optional)

Dow Corning Urethane Bond Glue

Procedure

1. Determine size of Masonite backing needed. Measure the height of 2 blocks plus the length of the mirror to determine the length of the backing. Measure the width of the mirror plus the width of 2 blocks for the backing width. Cut Masonite backing or have someone do it for you. Sand edges of backing board.

2. Center and glue mirror to backing board with mirror glue. (When the glass is properly placed, you will have a border around all sides wide enough for the block edging plus the frame.)

3. If wooden spools are not already painted, apply 2 coats of acrylic paint in a variety of colors or in colors to match the decor of the child's bedroom. (The easiest way to paint and dry wooden spools is to string them on a piece of wire and spray-paint them.)

4. Begin to line up mirror border, alternating blocks and spools around the 4 sides of the mirror. Glue to backing. (You can arrange blocks alphabetically, at random, or arrange them to spell a child's name.)

5. If you plan to paint framing, apply 2 coats of acrylic paint in the color of your choice. (You can purchase framing already finished, if you prefer.) Let paint dry. Spray with 2 coats of spray finish, allowing drying time between coats.

6. Glue sections of framing around the outside edges of the blocks and spools.

small piece of black felt
pair of old nylon stockings or panty hose
wide yarn
piece of string

Snake Pull-Toy

(See completed project on page 7.)

Not too long ago I made a pull-toy out of some old tin cans and it has become a favorite with the toddlers who accompany their mothers to our shop. The toy: a long snake with a tin can body filled with pebbles and covered with fabric. A local Scout troop has made this toy in quantity for a nearby children's home. It is a good gift for a Scout's little brother or sister, too.

Materials

**6 tin cans (use only cans with punctured top
   openings, not cans with lids removed)
pebbles
adhesive tape
fabric: long enough to cover all 6 cans with
   allowance for head; cut wide enough to
   encircle cans (allow some extra for seam) so
   that cans may be inserted easily when the
   fabric is seamed**

Procedure

1. Put a few pebbles in each can through the opening holes. Place adhesive tape over the holes. Stand on the cans to squash them in the middle. (Children love to do this!)
2. Fold fabric in half lengthwise, right sides together. Shape one end of the fabric for the snakes's tail by cutting the fabric on a diagonal, starting 4 inches from the bottom sides, and tapering to nothing at the bottom center fold. See *Diagram A.*
3. Sew the long side seams and the diagonal end seam. Leave the short straight end open for turning; when sewn, turn fabric to the right side (a yardstick helps to push the diagonal end up through the center of the fabric and out the opening edges).
4. Make a casing on the opening edges by turning down and sewing a ½-inch opening in the hem to insert a drawstring. See *Diagram B.*
5. From your fabric cut out 2 ears. From felt cut out 2 ear facings and 2 eyes. See *Diagram C.*
6. Placing right sides of fabric together (wrong sides up), sew ear facings to ears, leaving one end open for turning; turn ears to the right side; tuck in raw edges and sew open ends.
7. With the fabric side up (felt side down), center and sew ears 3½ inches from the opening casing edge and ½ inch apart. Center and sew eyes in place 3 inches from the casing edge and 1 inch apart. See *Diagram D.*
8. Stuff a nylon stocking down into the diagonal end of the fabric to give shape to the tail. Insert cans in fabric, one at a time; separate cans by tying bow with yarn around the fabric between each can. Stuff another nylon stocking into fabric after the last can has been inserted to give shape to the head.
9. Insert a piece of string through the casing opening, and draw the open ends together. Tie in a knot and cut the excess string.
10. Cut 3 pieces of yarn, each 40 inches long; braid to make a snake chain leash. Attach to the bow between the head and first can.
11. Make a tassel tail from yarn or buy one ready-made. With needle and thread, tack to the diagonal end of the fabric.

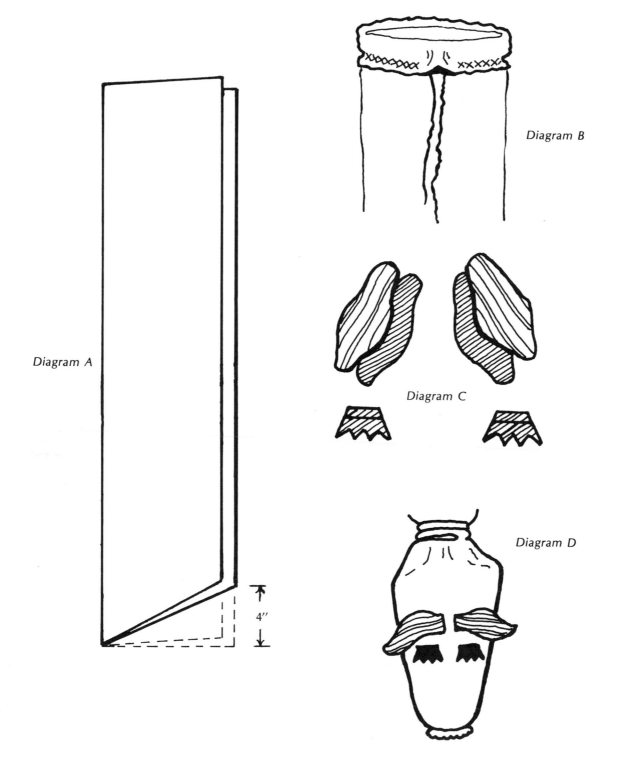

Diagram A

Diagram B

Diagram C

Diagram D

4"

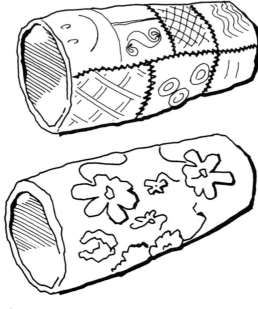

Electrical Cord Holder

(See completed project on page 173.)

Organizing kitchen drawers presents a problem for most or us. If you have trouble keeping electrical appliance cords in order, don't throw away cardboard tissue rolls. Covered with Sculptamold for texture and decorated with decoupaged paper napkins for color, they'll keep your electrical cords handy and orderly.

Materials

Sculptamold
white glue
cardboard tissue roll
old bread and butter spreader
decoupage sealer or acrylic spray
acrylic paint, brush-on or spray, in color of your choice
instant decoupage (Fun Podge, Mod Podge, Decollage)
3-ply paper napkins with printed designs or cutouts from wallpaper, gift wrapping paper, or fabric

Procedure

1. Mix a small portion of Sculptamold at a time, according to directions on the package (it sets up for working in 30 minutes, and dries quickly); add white glue for added strength. Spread on outside of cardboard roll with a bread and butter spreader, keeping texture rough. (If Sculptamold is not available, use papier-mâché, but add more glue and allow more drying time.)
2. Apply a coat of decoupage sealer or acrylic spray inside and outside the cardboard roll. Let dry.
3. Apply 2 coats of acrylic paint inside and outside the roll, allowing drying time between coats.
4. Brush instant decoupage inside and outside the roll. Let dry.
5. Pull out the top design layer from a 3-ply paper napkin. Plan where you will place the design on the roll. Pull off excess paper at back seam; this seam will not show when the paper is glued. (If you are using wrapping paper, wallpaper, or fabric, cut out your designs and plan placement on cardboard.)
6. Place napkin on the roll. Brush a coat of instant decoupage over the napkin; let dry. (The sheer napkin will allow the acrylic base color to show through.) If you are using paper or fabric cutouts, brush instant decoupage on the back of the cutouts. Glue down cutouts; let dry.
7. Apply a final protective coat of instant decoupage to the cardboard roll.

VARIATION 1: As a substitute for procedure 5, paint designs on cardboard roll in a vari-colored patchwork pattern, using lines and circles and "squiggles" for a whimsical free-form design. Apply coat of instant decoupage.

VARIATION 2: Cut up a paper towel cardboard roll into napkin rings; apply a coat of glue before cutting to prevent splitting. Proceed as above.

Crystallized Pin Tray

(See completed project on page 3.)

Procedure

1. Separate carrot leaves into tiny pieces. Separate floral sprig into individual flowers and remove stems.

2. Place crystals in the pie plate to a depth of ¼ inch. Place carrot leaves and flowers at random. Preheat oven to 375 or 400 degrees. Place plate in oven; heat for 10 to 15 minutes for a bubbly texture or for 20 to 30 minutes for a smooth glass-like texture. (A slight chemical odor is given off while the crystals are heating; ventilate your room. Crystals are perfectly safe in your oven, but do not place them near a flame or a broiler.) Remove from oven and cool.

3. When cool, remove tray from pie plate.

Makit and Bakit is a relatively new craft product, made up of plastic crystals that, when heated in a mold in the oven, change to a gum-like substance; then as the substance cools, it hardens to resemble stained glass. Makit and Bakit comes in a variety of colors, and can be made into jewelry, mobiles, Christmas tree ornaments, and more.

In this project I have used clear Makit and Bakit crystals, fresh carrot leaves, and tiny pink and white velvet flowers from a package decoration to create a pretty crystal-like pin tray for my dresser. My mold was a Pyrex pie plate, but a stainless steel or aluminum mold will do just as well.

Materials

fresh carrot leaves
small velvet flowers
clear Makit and Bakit crystals
Pyrex pie plate or stainless steel or aluminum mold, approximately 9 inches in diameter

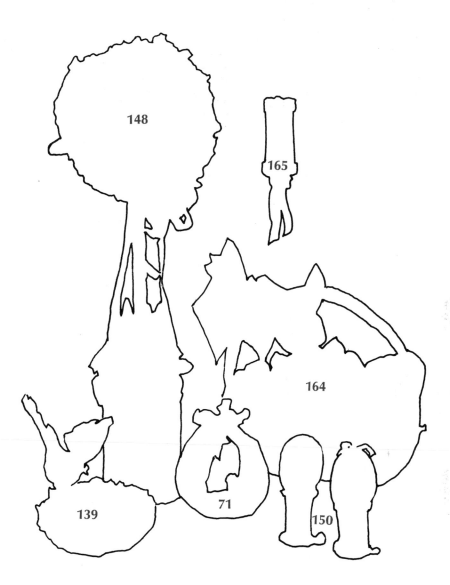

Details and instructions for projects shown may be found on page number indicated

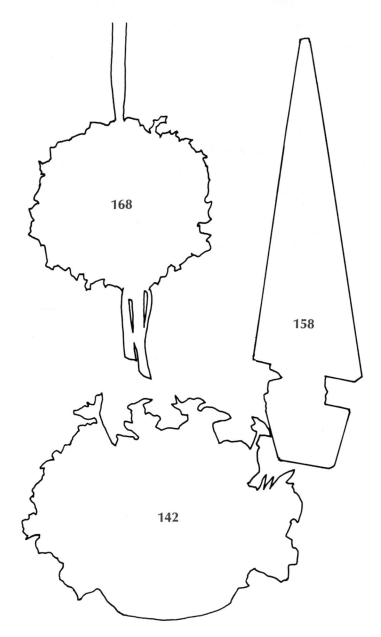

Details and instructions for projects shown may be found on page number indicated

Chapter
5

For the Holidays

Dove of Peace Ornament
Topiary Tree
New Year's Eve Centerpiece
Easter Egg Tree
Santa Claus Starfish
Shopping Bag Plaque
Plastic Bag Easter Topiary Tree
Decorative Eggs
Christmas Placemats
Springtime Door Decoration
Thanksgiving Dessert Plates
Santa Paperweight
Bleach Bottle Snowman
Wishbone Ornament
Thanksgiving Cornucopia
Bottle Cap Christmas Tree
Plastic Bag Wreath
Coffee Can Lid Ornament
Straw Wreath
Easter Party Napkin Decoration
Pill Bottle Ornament
Santa's Boot Cookie Container
Kissing Ball

Procedure

1. Mix a small amount of wallpaper paste, according to directions on the label.
2. In a *deep* bowl, make a half-and-half mixture of wallpaper paste and glue.
3. Submerge a handful of excelsior or straw into the mixture and wring out excess paste.
4. Mold straw into an upside-down nest shape over the top of an empty spray can. When it begins to set, lift off the nest and turn any loose ends over into the inside nest. Let dry face up at room temperature. (If you're making a quantity of nests, dry them on a cookie sheet in a low oven.)
5. Glue a pinch clothespin underneath the nest to attach it to the tree.
6. Spray the inside and outside of nest gold; let dry.
7. Insert a dove into the nest, if the bird's feet are wired, or glue the feet in place.
8. Glue 3 pearls—for eggs—in the center of the nest.

VARIATION: If you prefer a natural nest, omit the gold spray and attach a cardinal instead of a dove.

Dove of Peace Ornament

(See completed project on page 134.)

Don't throw away the excelsior or straw-like material that comes in some packing boxes. Use it to make a nest for a peace dove, and hang this appropriate ornament from your Christmas tree. You may even consider decorating your entire tree with these miniature nests.

Materials

wallpaper paste
deep bowl
white glue
excelsior or packing straw
empty spray can
pinch clothespin
gold spray paint
artificial white dove
3 imitation pearls

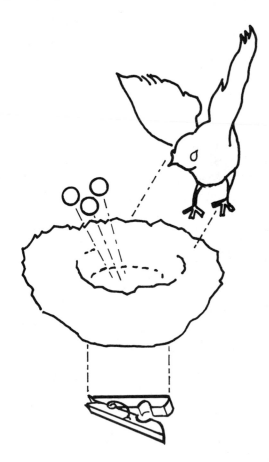

140

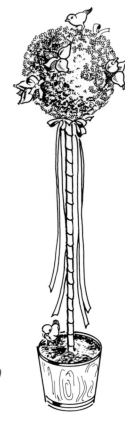

Topiary Tree

(See completed project on page 57.)

A topiary tree is the most versatile of all decorations. It can be small enough to be used as decoration for a coffee table or an individual place setting, or large enough to stand outside your front door. It can be kept without decoration, or decorations can be added or changed to match the seasons, celebrations, or holidays.

For a large topiary (such as the one described here), use an old mop or broom handle. For a smaller topiary, use a small dowel, such as the type attached to scrubbing sponges.

Materials

Styrofoam ball in size of your choice (mine was 6 inches in diameter)
green acrylic spray paint (check label to be sure paint won't disintegrate Styrofoam; do not use enamel paint)
green florist tape
old mop or broom handle or dowel: length and width of your choice, in proportion to size of ball (mine was 36 inches high)
3 yards moss green velvet ribbon, 1½ inches wide (you will need more or less, depending on the size of your topiary; you might choose a narrow ribbon for a smaller topiary)
white glue
small bag of plaster of Paris
small rocks or stones
metal can (I used a paint bucket and removed the handle; use a vegetable can for a smaller topiary)
flowerpot into which metal can will fit
small flat pieces of Styrofoam, including piece to fit inside top of metal can
Stickum
moss
U-shaped pins, T-straight pins, or hairpins
artificial boxwood or any greens of your choice
artificial pears and partridges
3 yards velvet ribbon, 1 inch wide, in color of your choice (for bow)
fine wire

Procedure

1. Spray Styrofoam ball with misty coats of green paint until covered; let dry.
2. Wrap green florist tape around the outside of the ball to divide it in half, then around again to divide it into 4 equal sections. (This will enable you to divide your greens evenly and center your dowel so that the topiary is balanced and will not topple.)
3. Wind handle or dowel with green florist tape, pulling tightly as you wind so that the velvet ribbon will not slip when attached.
4. Wind handle or dowel with velvet ribbon; you'll get a rippled, rough look in ribbon as you wind it. Attach at the beginning and end with a little glue.
5. With a sharp pair of scissors, make a small hole in the center bottom of the ball where the tape crosses. Through this hole insert the ribbon-covered dowel halfway up into the Styrofoam. Remove the dowel; insert a little glue into the hole, and again insert the dowel.
6. Mix a small quantity of plaster of Paris according to directions on the label. Put a few layers of rocks or stones into the bottom of the metal can to weight it. Fill three-quarters of the can with plaster of Paris. When almost set, insert the bottom of the dowel into the center of the plaster. Step back and survey

to see that it's straight; make any necessary adjustments before permitting plaster to harden.

7. Insert metal can and topiary into the flowerpot. Wedge small pieces of Styrofoam down into the open area between the 2 containers. Cut 2 pieces of Styrofoam to go around dowel hole, which together will be slightly smaller than the diameter of the top of the flowerpot. Fit in across the plaster, with Stickum between the Styrofoam and the plaster.

8. Cover the Styrofoam with moss attached by U-shaped pins, T-straight pins, or hairpins.

9. Divide artificial greens into 4 piles. Begin to insert them into the Styrofoam ball, placing a piece in one section, then a piece in another section, rotating placement around the ball so that you have even balance at all times. Continue placing greens until all open areas are covered.

10. Insert artificial pears into the ball. (Be sure to divide them first into 4 piles as you did the greens.) For pears without stems, heat an ice pick, make a hole in the fruit, and insert a wire stem into the hole.

11. With your velvet ribbon, make a bow with 2 long ribbon streamers; wire bow to the dowel at the base of the trimmed Styrofoam ball. You can also use your ribbon to make small wired bows to fill in any area on the ball where greens are scanty.

12. Insert one partridge into the top of the Styrofoam ball and the other into the flower container or wire it to the base of the dowel.

VARIATIONS: You can change the decorative items on your topiary tree each month of the year, if you wish. Simply remove the partridge and the pears, and use one or more of the following suggestions, or the decoration that best suits your decor.

January: lemons and oranges
February: red velvet tubing, hearts, and net
March: shamrocks and leprechauns
April: jelly beans, eggs, and bunnies
May: spring flowers or flags for Memorial Day
June: roses
July: firecrackers and flags
August: daisies
September: apples and corn
October: pumpkins and scarecrow
November: fruits and Pilgrims
December: Christmas tree balls and Santa; or red velvet roses, holly, and Santa

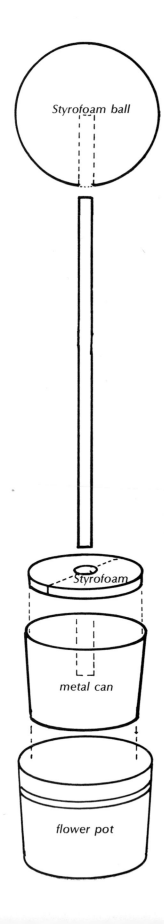

New Year's Eve Centerpiece

(See completed project on page 137.)

We don't usually think of a special decoration for New Year's Eve, but I think if you're giving a party, it's nice to provide a centerpiece just for the occasion. This decoration combines dried Queen Anne's lace sprayed with paint and sprinkled with diamond dust with fresh greens and a felt clock. It is especially beautiful when flanked by lighted candles.

Materials

Queen Anne's lace
soft brush
white acrylic spray paint
silver pearl spray paint
diamond dust
Velverette Craft Glue
fresh fine-foliaged greens
florist oasis
container for centerpiece
Styrofoam circle, ¾ inch thick and 2½ inches in diameter
scraps of red and white felt
very thin gold string braid
India ink
8 black round-headed pins
small red bead or sequin
corsage pin
stiff wire or stem

Procedure

1. Bring some Queen Anne's lace indoors when blossoms are tight. Air-dry at room temperature. Brush out tiny seed pods with a soft brush.

2. Spray Queen Anne's lace with white paint. Spray again with pearl paint (or another coat of white paint) and sprinkle on diamond dust while the paint is still wet.

3. Apply diluted Velverette Craft Glue to the greens; lightly sprinkle diamond dust over the greens.

4. Cut oasis to fit the container you plan to use and soak it in water. Place oasis in container; you may wrap it in aluminum foil or plastic wrap to protect your container, if necessary. Arrange greens and Queen Anne's lace in the oasis, keeping the latter above the greens in the arrangement.

5. Sand or file the edges of Styrofoam circle on both sides so that it resembles the convex shape of a clock.

6. Cut a red felt circle 3 inches in diameter. Glue red felt circle to one side of Styrofoam clock, and turn the extra ½-inch edge toward the other side. (See diagram.)

7. Cut a white felt circle 2¼ inches in diameter; glue to the other side of the Styrofoam, covering the red felt turnover edges. Let dry.

8. Glue a thin gold string braid around the outside edge of the clock and around the outside edge of the white felt.

9. With India ink, print the quarter hours on the white felt in Roman numerals: III, VI, IX, and XII. Draw the hour and minute hands to a few minutes after twelve. Cut black pins to a ½-inch length and insert as markers for the remaining hours on the clock.

10. Glue a small red bead or sequin to the clock center where the hands meet.

11. Insert a corsage pin—for the clock stem—into the center top of the clock.

12. Insert a stiff wire or stem into the bottom of the clock and insert the clock into the oasis.

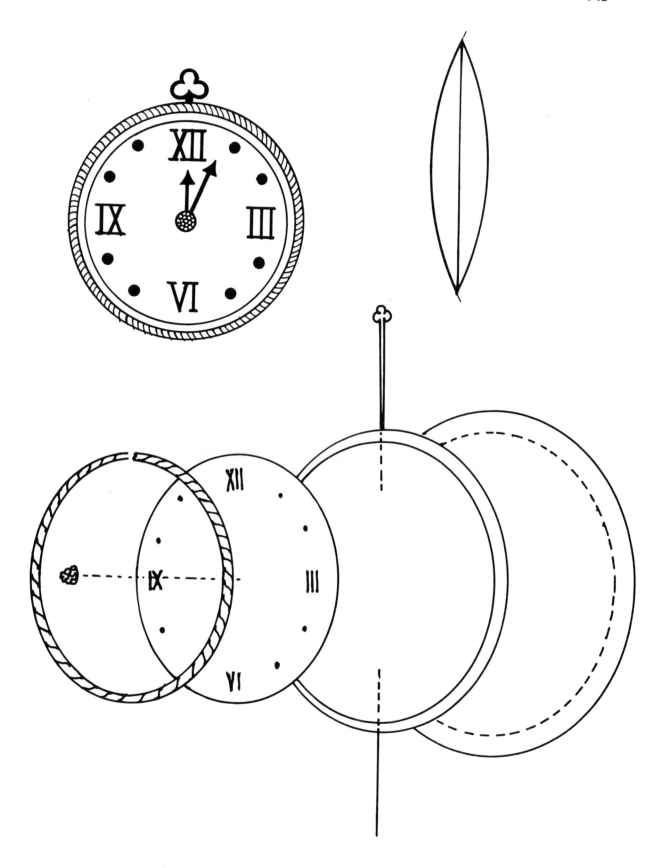

small tree branch (or a manzanita
    branch—available at craft stores and florists)
small flat pieces of Styrofoam, including piece to
    fit inside top of container
Stickum
moss
U-shaped pins, T-straight pins, or hairpins
plastic eggs (soft enough to insert pins) or
    Styrofoam eggs if plastic is not available in
    white or colors of your choice
acrylic paint, brush-on or spray, in colors of your
    choice (optional)
egg dye (optional)
bits of fabric, braid, lace, rickrack, ribbon, felt
old jewelry, single earrings, beads, pearls,
    sequins
miniature figures of your choice
pins: straight, corsage, jeweled
decoupage or manicure scissors (optional)
clear nylon thread
artificial trim of your choice for tree base, such
    as a bunny, flowers, jelly beans
delicate flower blossoms (optional)
1 yard narrow velvet ribbon in color of your
    choice (optional)

Easter Egg Tree

(See completed project on page 108.)

When my grandson, Scott, was born on Good Friday, I sent an egg tree instead of flowers. The plastic eggs on the tree were decorated with mementos of our family's life: my mother's pearls and earrings, lace from an old christening gown, lace from Scott's mother's wedding gown, buttons and trimmings from some old family dresses, braid from family chair upholstery. The possibilities for decorating an egg tree are endless (see suggestions in "Procedure"). It's a wonderful project for the whole family to undertake, and you can add to it as the years go by.

Materials

small bag of plaster of Paris
plastic flowerpot or decorative container of your
    choice (if you use decorative container that
    isn't plastic, you'll need a metal can to fit
    inside container)

Procedure

1. Mix a small quantity of plaster of Paris, following directions on the label. Fill three-quarters of plastic flowerpot or metal can.
2. When plaster is almost set, insert the tree branch into the container, making sure it is straight. Let plaster dry and harden.
3. If you use a metal can, insert it into your decorative container and wedge small pieces of Styrofoam down between the containers. Cut out a piece of Styrofoam to fit over the plaster in the flowerpot or metal can and insert into the container, with Stickum between the plaster and the Styrofoam.
4. Cover the Styrofoam with moss attached by U-shaped pins, T-straight pins, or hairpins.
5. Start work on the eggs at your leisure long before you plan to use them. Collect bits and pieces of family treasures. Ask for family contributions; you may be surprised at some of the ideas that come your way when you view your collection. Here are some of the ways you might trim your eggs: a) Paint a white plastic egg any color, or dye it with egg dye. b) Paint a patchwork egg with

various colors of acrylic paint. c) Paint the design of your choice in the color of your choice on an egg. d) Paint a face on an egg; add a felt or ribbon scarf or a miniature party basket decorated with flowers turned upside-down for a hat. e) Decorate an egg with braid or lace and attach by inserting straight pins through the opening in a pearl or bead. f) Cover an egg completely with fabric or lace. Cut the fabric into 2 circular pieces; attach one of the circles around half of the egg by inserting straight pins through the fabric into the egg. Attach the other circle to the remaining half of the egg with pins, overlapping the fabric at the center seam. Cut away excess fabric and cover the seam line with narrow ribbon. g) Paint an egg and then make a cross with tiny pearls attached with straight pins. h) With decoupage or manicure scissors, cut the egg into a basket shape and fill with tiny pearl eggs or the miniature figure of your choice, such as a chicken or bunny.

6. Fasten eggs at the center top with a double knotted length of clear nylon thread attached to a corsage pin or a jeweled pin. Hang at random on the tree.

7. Make a grouping under the tree with the Easter decoration of your choice: jelly beans, a bunny, flowers. Insert into the Styrofoam or wire to the tree branch.

8. *Optional:* Attach small delicate blossoms to the tree branch.

9. *Optional:* Tie narrow velvet ribbon around the flowerpot or decorative container. Make a bow at the center front.

Santa Claus Starfish

A starfish brought home from a seashore vacation and dried in the sun can be made into a unique Christmas ornament. My grandchildren found some starfish already dried on the beach and made this Santa Claus ornament for their Christmas tree.

Materials

starfish
red, white, and black acrylic paint
spray finish
ice pick
clear nylon thread

Procedure

1. Dry starfish outdoors in the sun (do not dry in the house).

2. Paint Santa's mouth, nose, hat, and suit red. Paint the beard and the fur on the hat, pants, and coat sleeves white. Paint the eyes, belt, gloves, and boots black. Do not paint the skin area. Let paint dry.

3. Apply 2 coats of spray finish over the paint.

4. Make a small hole in the hat with an ice pick and insert a doubled knotted nylon thread for hanging.

Shopping Bag Plaque (See completed project on page 83.)

Ideas and materials for craft projects turn up in unexpected places (which is part of the fun). A year ago I saved several of the Christmas shopping bags designed for B. Altman's, a New York City department store. I couldn't bear to throw the bags away because they were printed with an absolutely charming Beatrix Potter design of mice scampering through a house on the night before Christmas. Later I decided to use them to make a holiday plaque.

Even though you won't have this particular shopping bag design to work with, you are going to learn here how to take several copies of the same print, cut out parts from some of the prints, and, applying the technique of dimensional decoupage, make an unusual holiday decoration to cherish for many years to come.

Materials

#220 sandpaper
wooden tavern sign, 16 inches × 21 inches × ¾ inch (available in craft shops)
decoupage sealer
red and green acrylic brush-on paint
decoupage or manicure scissors
2 shopping bags, each stamped with 2 identical prints, or 3 or 4 identical prints of your choice—perhaps from gift wrapping paper or old calendar prints
Velverette Craft Glue
Dow Corning Silicone Sealer
black thread (optional)
spray finish

Procedure

1. Sand tavern sign well. Seal both sides with decoupage sealer; let dry.

2. Brush on 2 coats of red acrylic paint over both sides of the wood, allowing drying time between coats. If your tavern sign has a routed decorative edge, paint the edge green. Print "Merry Christmas" in green at the top of the sign. (If you can't print, use a stencil or trace newspaper or magazine letters.)

3. With decoupage or manicure scissors, cut out one entire print. (I cut out the mouse house from one side of the shopping bag.) With one hand, hold the scissors pointed away from the print at a 45-degree angle; with the other, feed the print into the scissor blades. Center this base print on the wood and glue; let dry.

4. Examine your print. Decide which details, such as hair, clothing, objects held or being carried, parts of a scene that seem to come forward in the print, that you'd like to feature. Cut out these pieces from another print. (From my print, I cut out windows, doors, roofs, mouse faces and clothing, and house curtains.)

5. Shape your cutouts. If a cutout piece would curve inward in reality, hold it in the palm of your hand, face up, and gently push it into shape with the eraser end of a pencil or the flat of your fingernail. If a piece would curve outward, hold it in your hand, face down, to shape.

6. Squeeze silicone sealer onto the back of a cutout, pulling the tube away so that the glue resembles the peak of a beaten egg white. Use tweezers to help you pick up and place a cutout; place the cutout on the base print directly over the area that is the duplicate of your cutout. Let sealer dry. Continue in the same manner untill all cutout pieces are elevated for dimension in the picture.

7. Examine your print again to see whether there are any parts that might be given even more dimension. (Curtains can be given more fullness by elevating another layer of curtain. Houses can have exterior moldings elevated. Another layer of leaves can be added to a tree. With people, think of the outer-most clothing you wear; for example, an apron can be cut away from a dress and raised for fullness over the dress; a ribbon or hat can be elevated over hair.) Plan the elevation best suited to your picture; the more detail, the better. Cut out the pieces you need from your remaining prints for this added detail.

8. Shape cutouts in the palm of your hand, as in Procedure 5, and elevate them as in Procedure 6 over their duplicate areas on the cutouts you have already elevated. Let sealer dry completely.

9. *Optional:* If you have animal cutouts with whiskers, as I did, make dimensional whiskers by putting glue on black thread to stiffen it; cut to size needed and glue in place.

10. Apply 10 coats of decoupage spray finish for a high shine and for protection in the absence of a frame. Allow adequate drying time between coats.

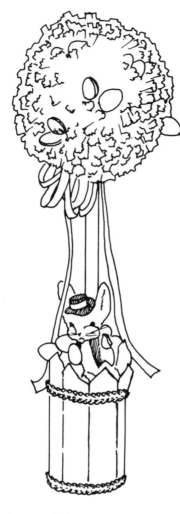

Plastic Bag Easter Topiary Tree

(See completed project on page 134.)

If you need a table centerpiece for a child's Easter party, make a topiary tree out of plastic sandwich bags, which you have *not* thrown away. This is an easy and inexpensive topiary to make.

Materials

dowel in length and diameter of your choice (I used a ½-inch-diameter dowel, 14 inches high)

acrylic paint in color of your choice (for dowel)

spray finish

plaster of Paris

metal can (I used a can 4½ inches high, 3 inches in diameter)

Styrofoam ball, 3 inches in diameter

green florist tape

clear-drying glue

50 to 75 plastic sandwich bags, or enough to completely cover Styrofoam ball

white pipe cleaners

plastic jelly beans on stems

small flat piece of Styrofoam to fit inside top of can

Stickum

moss

U-shaped pins, T-straight pins, or hairpins

2 yards narrow velvet ribbon in color of your choice

1½ yards velvet ribbon, 1½ inches wide, in same color as narrow ribbon (you may need more or less ribbon, depending on the size of the can you use)

guimpe braid to encircle can twice, in color of your choice

artificial bunny

Procedure

1. Apply 2 coats of acrylic paint to the dowel, allowing drying time between coats. When dry, apply 2 misty coats of spray finish and let dry.

2. Mix a small quantity of plaster of Paris, according to directions on the label. Fill three-quarters of metal can with plaster of Paris. When almost set, insert the dowel into the plaster, making sure it is straight. Let plaster dry and harden.

3. Find the center of the Styrofoam ball by wrapping green florist tape around the outside to divide the ball in half and then around again to divide it into 4 equal sections. With a sharp pair of scissors, make a small hole in the center bottom of the ball where the tapes cross. Insert the dowel halfway up into the Styrofoam through this hole. Remove the dowel, insert a little glue into the hole, and again insert the dowel.

4. Cut the side seams away from plastic sandwich bags. Cut each bag in half lengthwise and open out each cut strip to its full length. With your fingers gather each strip in the center; hold the gathers with your fingers as you gather 7 additional strips. Wind a pipe cleaner around the center of this bunch of plastic strips to hold the gathers together. See *Diagram A*. Using an end of the pipe cleaner as a stem, insert the bunch into one quarter-section of the Styrofoam ball.

5. Continue making bunches out of the strips and rotating placement in a different quarter of the Styrofoam ball so that you have even balance at all times. Continue until all areas of the ball are covered.

6. Insert plastic jelly beans into various sections of the ball, rotating placement to maintain even balance.

7. Cut flat piece of Styrofoam in 2 pieces to fit around dowel hole. Insert into the container with Stickum placed between the plaster and the Styrofoam.

8. Cover the Styrofoam with moss attached with U-shaped pins, T-straight pins, or hairpins.

9. With the narrow ribbon, make a bow with 9-inch streamers at both ends. Tie bow in the center with wire, and attach wire to the dowel at the base of the ball. Tie a "love knot" into each streamer 1½ inches from the bottom, by looping through once and pulling.

10. Cut wide ribbon into strips 1½ inches longer than the height of the metal can. Shape the top of the ribbon to form a 1½-inch-long upside-down V. See *Diagram B*.

11. Glue ribbon in vertical strips to the sides of the can, overlapping edges, with the straight cut end of the ribbon at the bottom of the can and the pointed edge at the top. See *Diagram B*.

12. Glue guimpe braid over the ribbon around the top and bottom edges of the can.

13. Insert plastic jelly beans into the moss at the base of the tree.

14. Insert an artificial bunny into the moss, or wire it to the bottom of the dowel.

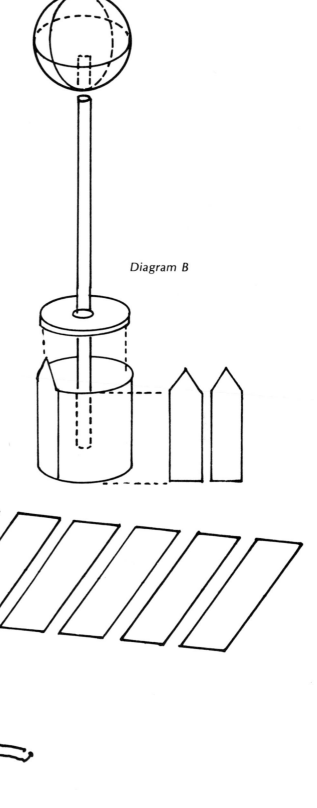

Diagram B

Diagram A

Decorative Eggs

(See completed project on page 134.)

Decorating eggs is a craft that calls for considerable artistry. But I'd like to show you an easy way to dress up the common chicken egg and have an exquisite Easter decoration. Hopefully, you'll make several eggs—to grace individual place settings or to give friends as a remembrance. Don't crack egg shells in the usual way when you're cooking with eggs; blow out the egg inside and clean and save the shell. And don't throw away gold caps on liquor bottles; combined with old curtain rings, they make perfect little bases for your decorated eggs.

Materials

chicken egg
corsage pin
awl
vinegar
decoupage or manicure scissors
instant decoupage (Fun Podge, Mod Podge, Decollage)

acrylic paint in color of your choice
diamond dust
Velverette Craft Glue
small piece of cotton (save cotton from pill bottles)
a few tiny dried flowers, a small piece of statice, or baby's breath
2 to 3 miniature figures of your choice (I used tiny pink bunnies)
leftover bits of narrow velvet ribbon
small bead or jewel or tiny decorative button
gold metallic braid
gold café curtain ring, approximately 1½ inches outside diameter (must be wide enough for top—open end—of bottle cap to fit inside)
gold spray paint, Liquid Leaf, or gold metallic wax (optional: if necessary to paint curtain ring)
decoupage sealer (optional: if necessary to paint ring
gold bottle cap from liquor bottle, large enough to hold egg

Procedure

1. Place the egg in warm (not hot) water for 10 minutes. With a corsage pin, make a hole in one end of the egg. With a clean awl, make a larger hole in the other end, and break the yolk with the awl. Let the egg drain out through this hole, then blow out any remaining egg. Wash the outside of the egg shell with a vinegar and detergent solution; if necessary, rub off stubborn stains with a plastic scouring pad and cleanser. Rinse the inside of the egg under the faucet. Drain and let dry completely.

2. With manicure scissors, make a hole in the center front of the shell. Carefully cut out an opening, according to the diagram.

3. Clean the inside of the egg shell well; let dry.

4. Brush one coat of instant decoupage inside and outside the shell; let dry.

5. Paint the inside and outside with 2 light coats of acrylic paint, allowing drying time between coats.

6. Brush one coat of instant decoupage inside the shell. While still wet, sprinkle diamond dust inside and shake it around to cover the entire area.

7. Glue a small piece of cotton to the inside bottom of the egg.

8. Cut tiny dried flowers, statice, or baby's breath to a 1-inch length. Put a bit of glue on the stems. Insert at various spots into the cotton.

9. Glue miniature figures onto the cotton.

10. Glue a piece of velvet ribbon vertically around the outside center of the egg, so that it covers the top and bottom holes. Make a tiny velvet bow and glue it over the ribbon at the center top; glue a small jewel, bead, or tiny decorative button to the center of the bow.

11. Glue metallic braid around the opening cutout edges of the shell.

12. If necessary, paint the curtain ring with gold spray paint, Liquid Leaf, or metallic wax, following directions on the label. Let dry. Apply one coat decoupage sealer over the paint.

13. Glue the closed end of the bottle cap into the center of the drapery ring.

14. Trim the top (open) outside edge of the cap and the outside edge of the ring with metallic braid. Set the egg into this base.

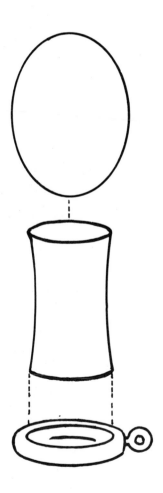

Christmas Placemats

So many of the Christmas cards we receive are too pretty to throw away. These holiday placemats are a good way to use them.

Materials

old placemats, poster board, or cardboard cut
　　from large gift boxes
Christmas cards
white glue
leftover fabric for back of cardboard or poster
　　board (optional)
acrylic spray

Procedure

1. If using old placemats, wash well and dry.

2. Plan composition of cards on placemats or cardboard. Cards can be cut, overlapped, arranged at odd angles. Glue them in place when you are satisfied with the grouping. Let glue dry thoroughly.

3. *Optional:* If you used cardboard or poster board, glue a piece of leftover fabric to the back of the cardboard.

4. Apply 3 misty coats of acrylic spray to the front and back of the placemats or cardboard, allowing drying time between coats.

VARIATION: Substitute birthday or Valentine's Day cards and make placemats for those occasions.

Springtime Door Decoration

(See completed project on page 170.)

Passers-by do get pleasure at the sight of a decorated front door, especially in spring or summer when they least expect it. Don't throw away a straw luncheon mat, a straw hat, or a wicker basket pocketbook. Fill one of these with flowers and brighten up your neighborhood. If you use fresh flowers from your garden, change according to what is in season.

Materials

straw luncheon mat (circular), woman's soft straw hat, or wicker basket pocketbook
pinch clothespins (optional: if using luncheon mat)
acrylic spray paint in color of your choice (optional: if using mat or pocketbook)
small rocks or stones (optional: if using pocketbook)
2½ to 3 yards water-repellent velvet ribbon, 1 inch wide, in color of your choice (for a bow with long streamers, you'll need additional yardage for weaving through the open areas of your mat or winding around the basket handle)
florist oasis (for fresh flowers) or Styrofoam (for artificial flowers)
moss to cover Styrofoam (optional: if using Styrofoam base)
U-shaped pins, T-straight pins, or hairpins
heavy-duty aluminum foil (for oasis)
bunches of fresh or artificial flowers
fresh or artificial greens of your choice
artificial decoration of your choice (optional)
wire

Procedure

1. a) If you are using a straw luncheon mat (as I did), soak it in water, bend it in half, and hold the 2 edges together at each end with pinch clothespins until dry; see *Diagram A*. When mat is dry, spray with 2 misty coats of acrylic paint, allowing drying time between coats. b) If you are using a hat, crush it in half, bend down one side so that the hat resembles an open envelope, and staple the sides together. See *Diagram B*. c) If you are using a basket pocketbook, remove the lid (if there is one) and spray pocketbook with 2 misty coats of acrylic paint. Weight the bottom with stones or rocks.

2. If you are using a mat, weave velvet ribbon in and out of the open areas around the mat, according to *Diagram C*. Start and end the ribbon at the center back of the mat.

3. a) If you use fresh flowers, cut a piece of oasis to fit inside your container. b) If you use artificial flowers, cut a piece of Styrofoam to fit inside container.

4. a) If you use Styrofoam, insert it into your container and cover moss attached by U-shaped pins, T-straight pins, or hairpins. b) If you use an oasis, soak it in water and wrap heavy-duty aluminum foil around all sides except the top. (When you are not using this decoration, you can remove the oasis, let it dry out, and soak it again when you are once more ready to use it.)

5. Cut flowers to desired length, and insert them into the Styrofoam or oasis. Fill in with fresh or artificial greens of your choice.

6. *Optional:* Wire on or insert an artificial decoration to achieve a focal point or celebrate the season—perhaps a butterfly or a bunny.

7. a) If you use a mat, tie the front and back center edges together with a long loop of velvet ribbon. b) If you use a pocketbook, wind velvet ribbon around the handle. c) If you use a hat, put fresh ribbon around the hatband and make ribbon streamers.

8. Make a bow with long streamers and wire it to the center front of the container.

9. Attach wire to your container (if you use a mat, conceal wire under velvet loop of ribbon) and hang from door knocker. If you have no knocker, drop wire down from top of door.

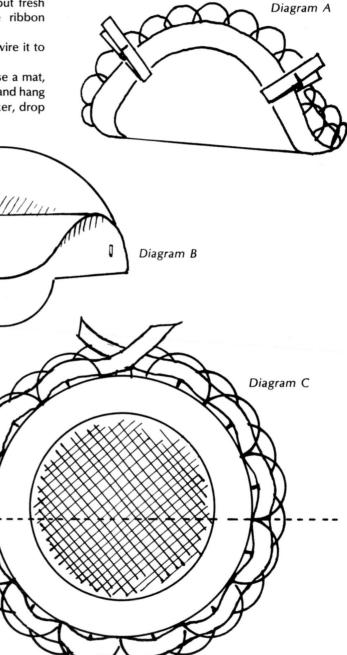

Diagram A

Diagram B

Diagram C

Thanksgiving Dessert Plates

(See completed project on page 3.)

Do you still have some of the glass salad or dessert plates that were so popular a few years back? And do you have any seed catalogs or calendars or greeting cards with pictures of luscious fruit? If so, you have the main ingredients for a handsome set of plates for that Thanksgiving pie, though, of course, these plates can be used for company dinners any time of the year. If you don't have the glass plates on hand, they are available at craft shops and dime stores.

A word of warning: Don't put these plates into a dishwasher. Wash and dry them carefully by hand.

Materials

clear glass plates, approximately 8 inches in diameter
ammonia
#0000 steel wool (optional: if necessary)
fruit prints (select a different fruit for each plate)

decoupage or manicure scissors
wax pencil or marking pencil
Decal-it*
decoupage paste
small soft sponge
Crackle-it*
Age-it* or antiquing stain in color of your choice
Liquid Leaf for gold plates, or antique white or flesh acrylic paint for antiqued ivory plates
Treasure Sealer or decoupage sealer (for gold plates only)
spray finish, clear varnish, or Protect-it*

These products are available together in a kit or may be purchased separately.

Procedure

1. Wash glass plates carefully with solution of soapy water and ammonia. If any spots remain, remove with #0000 steel wool. (Handle plates, as you work on them, with lint-free cloth or clean cotton gloves.)
2. Cut out the fruit prints carefully with decoupage or manicure scissors. Feed the paper into the scissors, keeping the curved point of the scissors away from the design at a 45-degree angle. Test each cutout print for size and appearance by placing it under a plate and looking at it through the front of the glass. With wax pencil or marking pencil, lightly draw guidelines on the front of the glass to indicate where the print will be glued. (These lines will show through to the back of the plate and can be wiped off when the print is attached.)
3. Mix a half-and-half solution of Decal-it and decoupage paste. Brush the mixture on the back of the plate and on the face of the print. Using the same pencil guidelines, position print on the bottom of the plate. Holding the plate so that you can see glue and air bubbles, work out all excess Decal-it from under the print by pressing and pushing it gently but firmly with your fingers, working from the center of the print out to each of the 4 corners. Be sure to remove every trace of glue, or you will have permanent spots on your plate.
4. With a soft sponge, stipple the excess Decal-it over the back of the plate. Let dry for 20 to 30 minutes; then apply 2 additional coats in the same manner, allowing 20 to 30 minutes drying time between coats. (When dry, the Decal-it will give an interesting textured look to your plate and will seal

the print to prevent subsequent paints and finishes from bleeding through.)

5. With your fingers, apply one coat of Crackle-it over the back of the plate. (The amount of Crackle-it you apply will determine the size of the cracks; use a smaller amount for finer cracks.) Let dry for at least an hour, longer if necessary. Fine cracks will form when coat is dry; you can usually see them if you examine the plate closely, although they will not become obvious until you apply an antiquing stain. If there are no cracks, apply a light second coat.

6. Apply one coat of Age-it or antiquing stain over the back of the plate and wipe off almost immediately. Some of the Age-it will stay in the cracks to emphasize them. Let dry for at least 24 hours.

7. Brush on 2 coats of Liquid Leaf for a gold finish or 2 coats of white or flesh acrylic paint to the back of the plate for an ivory finish; allow drying time between coats. You may prefer to add additional coats until the edges of the print cannot be seen. Be sure to let one coat dry completely before applying another.

8. If you used Liquid Leaf, apply a coat of Treasure Sealer or decoupage sealer over the back of the plate.

9. Apply 2 coats of spray finish, clear varnish, or Protect-it over the back of the plate. Wipe off wax pencil markings from front of plate.

10. Repeat entire procedure for number of plates desired, using different prints for each plate.

VARIATION: Make a set of Christmas plates, using different prints cut from Christmas greeting cards. Seal prints with Decal-it after gluing them to the plates; then paint the backs of the plates red or green.

Santa Paperweight

The favorite Christmas decoration made by the children in my junior craft class is a paperweight made from an instant coffee jar that they can shake to scatter snow over a minature Santa.

Materials

2-ounce instant coffee jar
ceramic Santa Claus, 2½ inches high
silicone sealer (good for use with water)
¼ teaspoon moth flakes

Procedure

1. Wash jar and lid; dry thoroughly.

2. Glue Santa to the inside lid with silicone sealer; let dry.

3. Fill jar with water. Put a scant ¼ teaspoonful of moth flakes into the jar.

4. Screw the lid on jar as tightly as you can. If the water level doesn't come to the top, add more water. If you need more flakes for an effective snow scene, add a small amount.

5. Open the jar and put silicone sealer around the edge of the lid. Screw lid tightly to the jar and let sealer dry.

156

Bleach Bottle Snowman

(See completed project on page 173.)
No matter what the weather is, you can make your own snowman with the help of an empty bleach bottle. You'll find he's a pleasant fellow to have around the house, not only as a Christmas decoration, but also as a winter doorstop or a decoration for a child's room.

Materials

1-gallon white plastic bleach bottle with handle
red ribbon to encircle middle of bottle, about 1½ inches wide
7 corsage pins
3 red buttons, about 1¼ inches in diameter
leftover string or yarn
dowel stick, 10 inches long and ¼ inch in diameter, or a thin, straight tree branch
ice pick or awl
sand
Styrofoam ball, 5 inches in diameter
white glue
small pieces of black moss fringe
2 black buttons, about ¾ inch in diameter
1 red wool sock
strip of green felt, 3 inches x 36 inches
small corncob pipe, inexpensive dime store pipe, or bubble-blowing pipe

Procedure

1. Consider the bottle handle the center back of the snowman. Wrap red ribbon around the middle of the bottle as a belt; overlap ends at the back and secure by inserting a corsage pin through the ribbon into the bleach bottle.
2. Place red buttons at the center front of the bottle, one above the belt and two below it; secure to the bottle by inserting a corsage pin through a button hole into the bleach bottle.
3. Make a broom for the snowman by looping string or yarn into 8 loops, each 3 inches long. Tie together at straight end—about ¾ inch in—with a piece of string, and attach to dowel stick or branch; cut loops.
4. With a heated ice pick or awl, make 2 holes in the bleach bottle wide enough to insert the dowel or branch; insert in the hole in the lower left side of the bottle and up through the upper right side hole.
5. Pour sand into the bottom of the bottle to weight the snowman.
6. With sharp scissors, make a hole in the center bottom of the Styrofoam ball that will fit over bleach bottle's top; make sure the fit is right by pushing ball onto bottle's top. Remove ball and put glue into the hole. Fit ball back on top of the bottle.
7. Make a snowman's face on Styrofoam ball. Glue on black moss fringe as a mustache. Insert corsage pins into a hole in each of the black button eyes and secure to the bottle.
8. Pull a red sock over the top of the Stryofoam ball as a stocking cap. Insert a corsage pin into the sock toe and secure it to the ball.
9. Tie green felt around the neck of the snowman as a scarf.
10. Make a hole large enough for the pipe with a heated ice pick or awl, and insert.

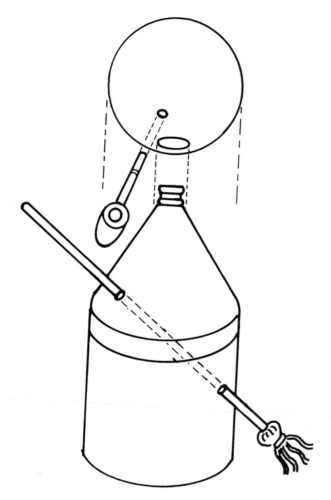

Wishbone Ornament

This is a good way to remember the happy family years: Save your Thanksgiving turkey wishbone, paint it gold, decorate it with rhinestones, and write the year on it with India ink. Do this after every Thanksgiving, and you'll soon have many wishbone ornaments to add real sparkle (and sentiment) to your Christmas tree.

Materials

turkey wishbone
ice pick
clear nylon thread
gold spray paint or Liquid Leaf
decoupage sealer
Dow Corning Urethane Bond Glue
rhinestones
India ink

Procedure

1. With ice pick, make a hole in the center top of the wishbone and insert a doubled, knotted clear nylon thread for hanging.
2. Spray or paint the wishbone gold, following directions on the label; let dry.
3. Apply one coat of decoupage sealer.
4. Glue rhinestones over the outside of the wishbone a small distance apart; let some of the gold show.
5. Write the year on the inside of the wishbone with India ink.

Thanksgiving Cornucopia

(See completed project on page 108.)

A traditional decoration for Thanksgiving is the cornucopia, or "horn of plenty." When I was growing up, the cornucopia was usually the Thanksgiving table centerpiece. If you have one stored in your home somewhere, don't throw it out. Refresh it with gold paint and renew the old plastic fruits or vegetables that used to go inside. The result will be a cornucopia much prettier than it was when brand new.

Materials

old cornucopia filled with plastic vegetables and
    fruits
woodtone spray, spray wood stain, or formula
    for Flemish flowers (Flemish flowers
    formula: 1 pint varnish, 1 pint turpentine, 1
    pint mahogany stain, ½ teaspoon burnt
    umber oil paint, and ½ teaspoon black oil
    paint)
gold spray paint
piece of Styrofoam
2½ yards velvet ribbon, 1½ inches wide, in color
    of your choice
gold wire

Procedure

1. Spray plastic fruit and vegetables with woodtone spray or spray wood stain, or dip in Flemish flowers formula and wipe with paper towel. Let dry.
2. Spray cornucopia gold; let dry.

3. Cut a piece of Styrofoam to fit inside the cornucopia and insert.
4. Insert fruit and vegetables into the Styrofoam and arrange attractively.
5. Make a full bow with velvet ribbon and wire it at the center. Attach the wire through the center top of the cornucopia.

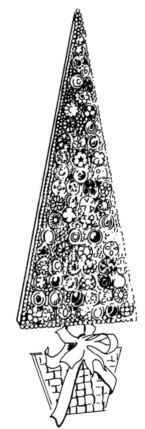

Bottle Cap Christmas Tree

(See completed project on page 137.)

We have a soft drink machine in our shop, and the wastepaper basket near it is always filled with bottle caps. It occurred to me that it should be possible to use those bottle caps instead of throwing them away. I had a Christmas tree form cut out of plywood; I glued the bottle caps, top down, onto the tree and filled the insides with old beans, buttons, and jewelry. I now have a shimmery, expensive-looking Chistmas wall or door decoration—straight out of the trash can!

Materials

piece of plywood or Masonite, approximately 30 inches × 9 inches × ¾ inch
#220 sandpaper
moss green acrylic paint
63 soda bottle caps with fluted edges (not screw-on type)
gold spray paint
pearls to go around edges of tree
Dow Corning Urethane Bond Glue
old buttons and jewelry, including beads, earrings, parts of bracelets and necklaces
Velverette Craft Glue or Dow Corning Silicone Sealer
3½ to 4 yards moss green velvet ribbon, ¾ inch wide

Procedure

1. Draw design for tree on plywood or Masonite, according to the diagram, and cut out with saw. Sand edges well. (You should have your local lumberyard perform this step if you are not accustomed to sawing wood.)
2. Spray or brush 2 coats green acrylic paint over both sides and the edges of the wood. Allow drying time between coats.
3. Remove cork from bottle caps. Turn the bottle cap tops down; spray the insides with several misty coats of gold paint; let dry.
4. Outline the edges of the tree (excluding the base and trunk) with pearls glued on individually with Dow Corning Urethane Bond Glue; let dry.
5. In the area of the tree inside the pearls, glue the bottle caps side by side in horizontal rows with the gold insides face up. Start at the bottom row; stagger the second row to fill in the open spaces in the first row; graduate to one bottle cap at the top row.
6. Fill the insides of the bottle caps with old jewelry and buttons. Work out a pattern; interchange placement until the arrangement pleases you. Then remove the jewelry and buttons from one cap at a time, put Velverette or silicone sealer into the bottle cap, and put back jewelry and buttons. Fill in all open areas between the bottle caps by gluing on pearls and odd beads. Continue until the entire area is covered.
7. Basketweave pieces of velvet ribbon to fit the area at the base of the tree. Cut to the shape of the tree base and glue in place with Velverette Craft Glue. (Try to keep from staining the velvet ribbon;

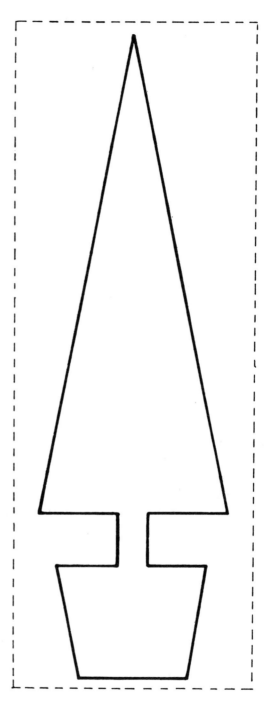

handle velvet as little as possible.) Let glue dry.
8. Glue velvet ribbon around the entire outside edge of the tree.
9. Make a flat velvet bow and glue it to the tree trunk.

soft and squishy, it will fit in the small space between an aluminum storm door and the house front door. If it gets soiled, it can be washed with soapsuds, and it will fluff up again, as fresh as new. So don't throw away plastic sandwich bags; save them and make a most versatile Christmas wreath.

Materials

plastic sandwich bags (straight bags—not bags with fold-over tops): approximately 150 if using coat hanger; approximately 200 if using regular ring
2 cardboard boxes
wire coat hanger, ring from old Christmas wreath, or 18-inch rippled ring purchased from craft store
2½ yards velvet ribbon 1½ inches wide, in color of your choice (use waterproof ribbon for outdoor use)
fine wire
lollipops
gold tinsel wire or narrow ribbon for tying on lollipops

Procedure

1. Place 4 or 5 plastic bags together, fold the bags in half *lengthwise,* and cut along the fold line. Fold again lengthwise, and cut along the fold line. (You'll have 4 strips for each bag.) Cut half of your bags this way. Put strips into one of cardboard boxes.
2. Place 4 or 5 whole bags together, fold in half *crosswise* (on the short side), and cut along the fold line. Fold again crosswise, and cut along the fold line. Cut rest of bags this way. Put strips into second cardboard box.
3. If using a coat hanger, cut off the handle. Pull the hanger into a circular ring shape.
4. Pick up one plastic strip at a time and tie it in a single tie around the ring (do not knot it); alternate 2 or 3 long pieces with 2 or 3 short pieces. Push the strips tightly together as you tie them. After adding several strips, give the pieces a twist to fluff them. Continue until the entire ring is covered.
5. Make a bow out of the velvet ribbon with 2 long streamers at either end. Wire it at the middle and tie it with this wire to the center top of the wreath.
6. Trim wreath with lollipops tied on with gold tinsel wire or narrow ribbon.

Plastic Bag Wreath

(See completed project on page 170.)

If you'd like to make an easy, inexpensive Christmas wreath, this plastic sandwich bag wreath is a good choice. It's shiny and pretty to look at and can be decorated in as many ways as your creativity can devise. I've decorated it with a red and green velvet bow and tiny sprigs of plastic vegetables for a kitchen; one year I tied pink velvet roses into the wreath along with a full pink velvet bow; for a child's room I've decorated it with lollipops (the version described here).

I'm quite fond of this wreath for many reasons. The basic wreath can be made far in advance of a holiday, put away, and trimmed later. Because it's

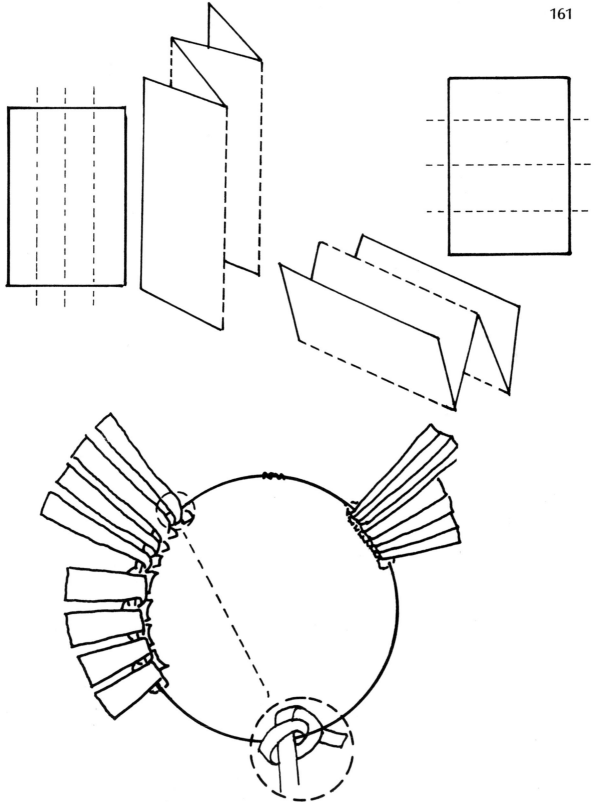

Coffee Can Lid Ornament

(See completed project on page 83.)

There are several leftovers and throwaways which make unusual and pretty tree ornaments. A plastic coffee can lid decorated with gift wrapping paper or a greeting card cutout is one.

Materials

plastic lid from 1-pound coffee, nut, or candy tin
cutouts from gift wrapping paper or greeting
    cards
instant decoupage (Fun Podge, Mod Podge,
    Decollage)
brayer
diamond dust
dimensional trim of your choice: button, ribbon,
    bead, or sequin (optional)
white felt to fit diameter of lid
Quik Glue or any other glue that adheres to
    plastic
narrow satin cording to encircle plastic lid
scalloped metallic braid to encircle plastic lid
gold string or clear nylon thread

Procedure

1. Cut away overlap rim from plastic lid.
2. With a pencil, trace outline of lid on cutout. Cut out picture slightly smaller than outline, to fit lid.
3. Brush a coat of instant decoupage over the top of the lid; let dry.
4. Brush another coat of instant decoupage over the top of the lid and over the back of the cutout. Press wet cutout in place on lid and, using a brayer covered with a dampened paper towel, press out excess decoupage by rolling from the center out to each corner. Let dry.
5. Brush another coat of instant decoupage over the top of the lid. While wet, sprinkle diamond dust over the lid; let dry.
6. *Optional:* Glue on dimensional trim, if it fits in with your picture, such as a tiny ribbon bow, a small decorative button, a bead, a star sequin.
7. Trace outline of lid onto white felt; cut out and glue to the back of the lid.
8. Glue narrow stain cording around outside back edge of lid so that a border shows on the front side.
9. Glue metallic braid around outside back edge of lid so that it covers the cording on the back and shows above it on the front as an edging.
10. Make a hanger by tying a knotted doubled piece of gold string or clear nylon thread through the braid.

Straw Wreath

(See completed project on page 170.)

A Christmas wreath is usually made with greens. But the wreath my students like to make is one made out of the ordinary straw that people put around shrubbery before winter sets in. The beauty of this wreath is its natural appearance. It is also very inexpensive. As with the topiary tree, the straw wreath can be trimmed to suit holidays other than Christmas.

Materials

newspaper to cover both sides of wire ring (amount depends on how thick you want wreath)
18-inch double wire ring (if you cannot get a wire ring, make one out of heavy cardboard, cutting it to an outside diameter of 18 inches and cutting away the center, doughnut fashion, so that ring is 3 inches wide)
straw or hay
strong wire or #28 gold wire
natural or artificial greens of your choice
3½ yards velvet ribbon, 1 inch wide, in color of your choice (water-repellent for outdoor use)
seasonal trim of your choice

Procedure

1. Fold each sheet of newspaper (a double page spread) in half lengthwise, then fold again into quarters.
2. With the help of a partner, wrap newspaper around the area between the inside opening and the outside edges of the ring, and wire it in place. (Let one person wrap newspaper and another wrap wire.) Keep overlapping the paper as you wrap. Keep applying newspaper to ring until you have achieved the thickness you desire.
3. Using the same winding technique, wire a bunch of straw or hay over the front of the ring on top of the newspaper, trying to achieve a rustic look. When all the newspaper on the front is covered, wire hay or straw to the back of the ring.
4. Tuck greens of your choice into hay on bottom part of wreath, or wire them in place.
5. Cut a piece of wire and wrap it around the entire top of the wreath for hanging. Make a bow with the velvet ribbon, leaving the ends long. Wire bow to wreath at the bottom.
6. Wire, tie on, or insert decoration of your choice into the center bottom of the wreath.

VARIATION: Between Procedures 3 and 4, spray with misty coats of gold paint, allowing drying time between coats, until you achieve the coverage you desire. Let dry before inserting greens.

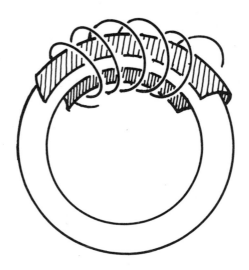

Easter Party Napkin Decoration

(See completed project on page 134.)

Even if you're not as skillful with your hands as some, you'll be able to make this Easter decoration. Tear off the designs on a leftover Easter party paper napkin, attach them to a Styrofoam egg with instant decoupage, and you'll have an egg pretty enough to leave on display long after Easter. Make several eggs and display them in a bowl or basket.

Materials

strong wire

Styrofoam egg in size of your choice

instant decoupage (Fun Podge, Mod Podge, Decollage)

2-ply party paper napkin with a not-too-large Easter design

diamond dust

2 corsage pins (optional: for standing up the egg)

large button with 2 holes (optional: also for standing up the egg)

Procedure

1. Insert a piece of wire into the egg as a holder while you work on it.

2. Brush a coat of instant decoupage over the entire egg; let dry.

3. Tear (do not cut) the Easter designs away from a party napkin, and tear the remainder of the napkin into small pieces. Pull apart and separate the 2 thicknesses of paper.

4. Brush a coat of instant decoupage of half the Styrofoam egg. While it is still wet, center largest paper Easter design on the egg and brush over the top of it with instant decoupage. Plan placement of smaller designs on same half of egg and brush them in place with instant decoupage. Fill in remaining areas on the egg with small pieces of the plain, torn paper, brushed on with instant decoupage. (Don't worry about ripped seam edges; they won't show when the egg has dried.)

5. Repeat the procedure on the other half of the egg, brushing on pieces of paper until the entire egg is completely covered with paper. Let dry.

6. Brush on another coat of instant decoupage over half of the dry egg. While the egg is still wet, sprinkle on diamond dust and let dry. When dry, turn the egg and repeat on the other half.

7. Remove wire.

8. *Optional:* If you want your individual egg to stand up, insert 2 corsage pins through the holes of a large button and insert the pins into the end of the egg.

Pill Bottle Ornament

(See completed project on page 134.)

Don't throw away a plastic pill bottle. Trimmed with a pretty button, bits of velvet ribbon, and a miniature figure, it makes a whimsical decoration for your tree.

Materials

plastic pill bottle
small piece of felt
Dream Puff or fine cotton
miniature of your choice (angel, Santa, religious
    scene, Christmas tree, toy, or reindeer)
Velverette Craft Glue (optional)
diamond dust or artificial snow (optional)
narrow velvet ribbon
fancy button
narrow gold braid

Procedure

1. With pencil, trace outline of lid top and bottle bottom onto felt. Cut felt to fit. Glue in place to the outside top of the lid and outside bottle bottom. Turn the bottle upside down and remove the lid. (You will be gluing your decoration into the inside of the lid, which will become the bottom of your finished ornament.)

2. Glue a small piece of Dream Puff or cotton to the inside of the lid. Glue a miniature figure on top of this cotton "cloud"; if you wish, extend the cotton up behind the miniature. If you use a Santa figure, apply diluted Velverette Craft Glue to cotton, sprinkle diamond dust or artificial snow over the cotton; then glue on Santa. Put bottle back onto lid.

3. Glue narrow velvet ribbon around top of bottle and edge of lid. Make a bow with 3-inch streamers out of the remaining ribbon, and glue it to the center of the felt on the lid at the bottom.

4. Glue a decorative button to the top of the bottle over the felt; let dry.

5. Cut a 10-inch piece of narrow braid. Double it, overlap the ends, and glue them together. Glue to the center of the button as a hanger.

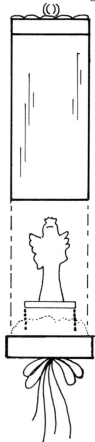

166

Santa's Boot Cookie Container

(See completed project on page 111.)

Finding a good container for a gift of home-baked Christmas cookies is sometimes difficult. Put your cookies in an old coffee can dressed up in a red felt boot. It will take only a small amount of fabric and a little extra time to dress up your gift, but good cookies are worth it.

Materials

1-pound coffee can with plastic lid
¼ yard red felt, 72 inches wide
pinking shears (optional)
tracing paper
cardboard
red thread
white pile fabric, 2 inches × 14 inches
white glue
6 eyelets and eyelet punch
white shoelace
tissue paper to stuff toe

Procedure

1. Wash empty coffee can well and dry thoroughly. Using a pencil, trace outline of lid onto red felt. Preferably with pinking scissors, cut out circle slightly smaller than outline. Center felt circle on outside of lid, glue in place, and set aside.

2. Draw the boot pattern pieces onto tracing paper to size you will need, and cut out. See *Diagram A*. Place on felt, and cut out one red sole, one toe and front piece, and one side and back piece (use pinking shears, if you wish); cut a cardboard sole according to the pattern, then trim off ¼ inch all around the edges.

3. Assemble boot; see *Diagram B*. Sew the toe and front piece to the front of the sole close to the edges, keeping edges even (sew by hand or machine). Sew the side and back piece to the back of the sole, keeping edges even and overlapping the front piece about 1 inch on both sides.

4. Glue or stitch the strip of white pile fabric over the outside top of the side and back piece, keeping top and side edges even. Trim away any excess fabric so that ends butt in front.

5. Make 2 eyelet holes in each side of the pile-covered felt ¼ inch in from the front edges and ½ inch down from the top. Space the holes about ½ inch apart. Make a hole in each side of the red felt ¼ inch in from the outside edge and ¼ inch down from the pile strip. (If you do not have an eyelet punch, cut 6 circular holes ¼ inch in diameter and edge them with a buttonhole stitch.)

6. Insert and lace a white shoelace through the eyelet holes.

7. Insert cardboard into the sole of the boot; stuff the toe with tissue paper. Insert coffee can into boot and fill with cookies. Put lid on can.

VARIATION: Embroider a small holiday motif on the front of the boot with crewel thread—maybe a sprig of mistletoe, a holly leaf, or a bell.

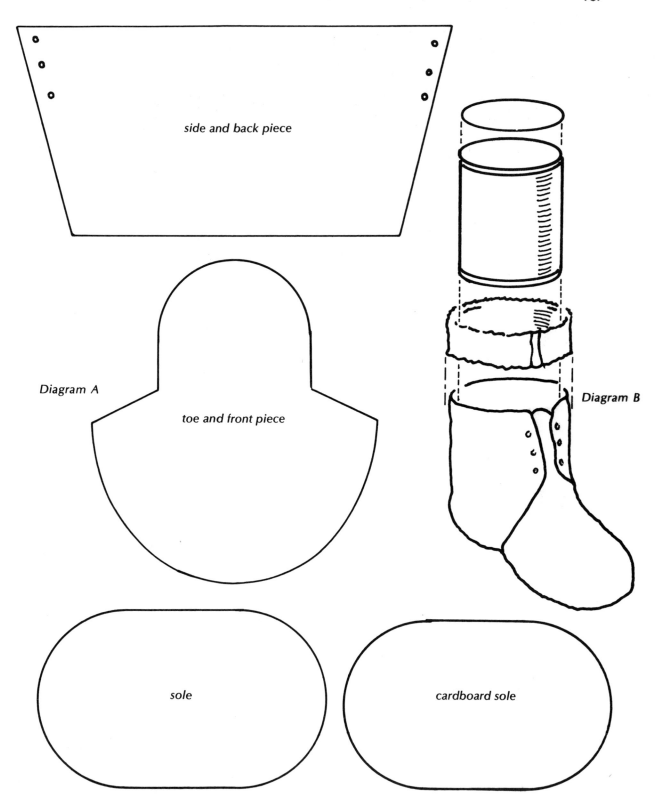

side and back piece

Diagram A

toe and front piece

Diagram B

sole

cardboard sole

Kissing Ball

Procedure

1. Submerge greens overnight in water.

2. Trim oasis to fit inside the 2 plastic boxes when they are placed together, with open ends meeting. Soak oasis in water.

3. Insert oasis in one of the boxes; turn the other box upside down over the oasis and wire the 2 boxes together on all 4 sides.

4. Insert greens into the oasis between the holes in the boxes. Trim the outside of your greens in a circular shape.

5. Insert into the oasis the holiday trim of your choice.

6. Make a bow of the ¼-inch ribbon and wire it to the top of the ball. Make several bows out of the same ribbon and wire them at random into the ball.

7. Make 2 long loops of the ¼-inch ribbon and attach them to the bottom of the ball. Tie mistletoe to these loops.

8. Insert a heavy hanging wire into the top of the ball, push it down through the bottom, and then bring it back up again. Twist the wires together at the top. Make a loop of wider ribbon and glue each side to the wire so that wire is hidden.

(See completed project on page 137.)

Don't throw away the square plastic boxes, with holes, in which cherry tomatoes and berries are sold. You can wire two boxes together to make a kissing ball. Fill this container with oasis, insert boxwood or holly and mistletoe through the holes, and hang the decoration from the center top of an entryway.

The greens in the kissing ball will stay fresh all through the holidays if you'll take down the ball after a few days, put it in the kitchen sink, add water to the oasis, and hang it again. Keep repeating as often as necessary.

Materials

greens of your choice: boxwood, holly, etc.

florist oasis

2 plastic produce boxes with small holes

heavy spool wire

holiday trim of your choice: tree ornaments, tiny sweetheart roses, etc.

red ribbon: ¼ inch wide for bows; 1½ iches wide for hanging

mistletoe

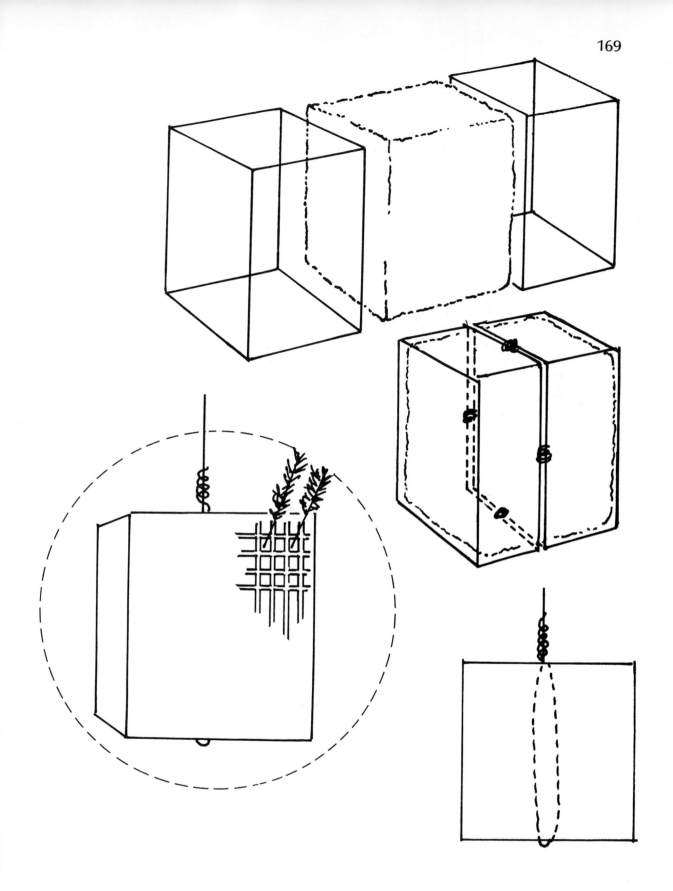